D1743952

# Emotional Intelligence

Control Your Emotions and Achieve Success in
Your Career and Personal Life

(Definitions, Models and Strategies for the Power
of Emotional Intelligence!)

**Linda Christensen**

Published by Kevin Dennis

**Linda Christensen**

All Rights Reserved

*Emotional Intelligence: Control Your Emotions and Achieve Success in Your Career and Personal Life (Definitions, Models and Strategies for the Power of Emotional Intelligence!)*

ISBN 978-1-989965-29-0

# Legal & Disclaimer

The information contained in this book is not designed to replace or take the place of any form of medicine or professional medical advice. The information in this book has been provided for educational and entertainment purposes only.

The information contained in this book has been compiled from sources deemed reliable, and it is accurate to the best of the Author's knowledge; however, the Author cannot guarantee its accuracy and validity and cannot be held liable for any errors or omissions. Changes are periodically made to this book. You must consult your doctor or get professional medical advice before using any of the

# TABLE OF CONTENTS

## Introduction

We all know the importance of the intelligence quotient (IQ). To rephrase that more aptly, I would say that we all know the importance attached to the intelligence quotient by certain schools and companies. It is made to seem like the ultimate measurement of an individual's potential. According to these schools and companies, the likelihood that a person would be innovative, creative, focused, and successful in any task can be determined by the level of their IQ. It has become clear and is more obvious with each day, that this is not the case. Some individuals who scored as high or higher than Einstein on their IQ tests did not perform as expected. They added very little to the advancement of their fields and sometimes failed to complete the tasks handed to them. Many poor people have been known to ace their IQ tests, while some wealthy individuals did not perform as glowingly. In fact, some of the more creative and innovative personalities in today's world did not score impressively on their IQ tests. So, what then is the defining factor? What can be used to determine a person's propensity for creative thinking, productive work ethic, and innovative behavior?

The problem is that we have been defining intelligence in a limited and, by extension, erroneous way. We glorify an individual's ability to reason, while conveniently overlooking the fact that not everyone who scores above average on these tests goes on to do great things with their lives. It takes a lot more to harness the potential in one's self and to deal with the various hurdles on the path to a successful life. It takes emotional intelligence, which can be shortened to EQ or EI. While the place of logical reasoning in the progression of society cannot be disregarded, the ace up the sleeves of leaders is the level of their emotional intelligence. This book will answer the many salient questions which surround EI and teach you to master your emotions. Each chapter is packed full of useful information and written in clear language for ease of reading. It is safe to say that the knowledge in this book will place you steps ahead of the majority of people who still look to the IQ as the be all for success.

## Chapter 1: The Impact of SOCIAL STYLE on Emotional Intelligence

Sara stormed into her office, practically slamming the door behind her. It had been another frustrating day. The deadline for the prototype of the new software application was just three weeks away and her team was way behind schedule to deliver its part of the program. She sat back in her chair and the more she thought about her team's failures the more upset she became.

Sara had recently been promoted into her first management position. She was now responsible for managing a small group of programmers whose job was to develop a critical component of GenRel's much-anticipated new introduction to the marketplace, the CapitalNet. This web-based application would link entrepreneurs with venture capitalists by using sophisticated algorithms that account for multiple factors and priorities of both parties. It would go much further than any other existing networking site in its capabilities and usefulness for this small but lucrative market.

But Sara's initial enthusiasm for the project was now turning into panic and anger. She simply couldn't understand why her staff was not responding to her leadership, not to mention the deadline. This was her first opportunity to prove that she could manage a team, and she was afraid she was about to fail in front of her peers and boss.

She got on the phone and called Mark, her former manager and long time mentor. Mark had taken her under his wing when Sara first joined the company after getting her M.B.A. He had taught her the business and had guided her through her initial years in the organization, teaching her all about the products and services, financials, and their marketplace. It was Mark, more than any other person, who had prepared her for moving into management.

Sara told Mark about the difficulties she was having with the members of her team: their lack of responsiveness to her requests, their failure to understand what she asked of them, the way they seemed to avoid meeting with her. Mark listened patiently and agreed to meet with her the next morning.

What Is Emotional Intelligence?

Before we discuss how SOCIAL STYLE is related to emotional intelligence, let's briefly review what EQ is all about.

Though some of the language of EQ is new, the concept is anything but. Interpersonal or social skill seems so important that it's hard to think of a time when people did not understand how critical it is for workplace effectiveness. However, beginning in the 1990s a collection of researchers and practitioners have had a major influence on the ways that people think about interpersonal effectiveness. Their achievements are most notable in two regards.

First, these researchers presented cohesive models of interpersonal competencies that were based on research. To that point, much of the research in this area had been scattershot and academic. In addition, some of these researchers have been very skilled at promoting their models, not only in academic outlets, but in the popular media as well. This has helped the EQ movement to become meaningful to wider audiences of people.

Second, an association of EQ theorists has steadily generated research showing evidence for the effectiveness of interpersonal skills.[1] Instead of rigidly sticking to their initial theories, most of the well-known EQ researchers have refined their models as new evidence becomes available. This has led to renewed interest in studying the impacts that interpersonal effectiveness has on organizations. These impacts include so-called soft measures, such as employee engagement and trust in leaders, and hard measures such as sales and revenue growth.

One of the most well-known EQ models in use today was developed by the psychologist and writer Daniel Goleman and his colleagues.[2] Along with other researchers, they have documented how people with high EQ outperform others in terms of yearly sales, success as managers and executives, and lower turnover rates. Further, they have shown the increasing importance that EQ plays as people progress in their careers and reach higher levels of management. At the highest levels within organizations, pure technical skill and intellectual ability are prerequisites, but they do not differentiate star performers from the rest as well as interpersonal abilities do.

Goleman's model is composed of four domains, divided into two areas of activity: personal competence (Self-Awareness and Self-Management) and social competence (Social Awareness and Relationship Management).

[1] Consortium for Research on Emotional Intelligence in Organizations. (2009). http://www.eiconsortium.org.

[2] Goleman, D. (1998). What Makes a Leader? Harvard Business Review, 76 (1), 93-102.

Emotional Intelligence Domains and Associated Competencies

Self-Awareness

• Emotional Self-Awareness

• Accurate Self-Assessment

• Self-Confidence

Self-Management

• Emotional Self-Control

• Transparency

- Adaptability

- Achievement

- Initiative

- Optimism

Social Awareness

- Empathy

- Organizational awareness

- Service

Relationship Management

- Inspirational leadership

- Influence

- Developing others

- Change catalyst

- Conflict management

- Building bonds

- Teamwork and collaboration

How Is Emotional Intelligence Related to SOCIAL STYLE?

For those of you who are experienced with TRACOM's SOCIAL STYLE Model™, the four domains of EQ should seem familiar. This is because they closely parallel the four steps for increasing interpersonal effectiveness that were developed by TRACOM in the 1960s:

• Know Yourself

• Control Yourself

• Know Others

• Do Something for Others

The four steps listed above are fundamentally related to Style. Our Styles influence how we behave in each of these areas, and therefore, Style heavily influences our effectiveness with others. Understanding behavioral differences will help you practice EQ behaviors more effectively.

Recent research has shown that EQ is highly related to Versatility.[1] This is not surprising considering the similarities between the two models, but it provides concrete empirical evidence that by increasing Versatility and Style awareness, people can also increase their EQ.

The following chapters are organized by each of the EQ domains. We discuss the competencies within each domain and describe how people of each Style tend to behave and be perceived by others. We then offer suggestions for how people of each Style can work more effectively with others.

In addition, we have included a section on how to work more effectively with people of each Style. This can be helpful when you are challenged in working with a specific individual.

To get the most out of this guide, we recommend that you read it through from beginning to end to understand the context of how Style is related to EQ. It can then be used as a convenient reference.

## Chapter 2: How a higher emotional intelligence can benefit your life

Now that you understand what EQ is, we can now discuss how it can help you in your life. When discussing EQ, we are discussing identifying and managing other people's feelings. So how can that make your life better you ask? Well first, you will be able to empathize with people rather than feel pity for them. Increasing your EQ knowledge will also benefit you when it comes to communicating with the people in your life and those that you interact with on a regular basis.

Learning how to be empathetic towards others will go a long way in making your connections to others better. By being empathetic you will increase your ability to control your emotions and those of others. Your increased knowledge of EQ will push you to become a better you in all our relationships.

Communication for many of us is merely the means of sharing information. However, there is so much more to good communication. Communication is not about only relaying information, but also actively listening and being able to be an active participant in the interaction. You learning how to become a better communicator will not only improve your interaction with others but also, your relationships and your EQ. Communication is a helpful tool that often gets overlooked in everyday life, as we tend to believe that if you can talk and 'listen' you are doing enough. This chapter will provide you with useful information for today and your future.

Empathy not pity

The word empathy typically brings up the age old saying to learn how to "put yourself in someone else's shoes." However, this could not be further from the truth. Empathy is about learning to see things from someone's point of view. It is more than just trying to feel what someone else is feeling, as you cannot truly do that. Rather it is about pushing yourself to ignore your own belief system and allow others to share what they are feeling with you. In other words, it is about trying to see things from someone else's perspective by gaining an understanding of what they are experiencing.

Unlike pity – where you in a sense feel sorry for them and their current circumstances – which does nothing to benefit the person, empathy allows you to help someone. Empathy allows a person to feel and be heard, while also knowing that someone understands their situation. Empathy is pushing you to let down your guard and let people feel and experience what they need to at that moment.

developing empathy

Now that you know what empathy is, how do you go about developing it? First, you must learn to let go of feeling bad for others. Feeling bad does not provide anyone with anything, rather it puts both parties in an uncomfortable exchange. Oftentimes, we feel bad for people because we do not know what else to feel. If you find yourself feeling bad for someone, ask yourself why? It may be that you are uncomfortable with their sadness and do not know how else to process those emotions. You may believe you cannot do anything else besides feel bad for their scenario.

However, this could not be further from the truth! By feeling bad about a person's situation, you only further take away their power. But, if you can provide them with support and truly listen and HEAR what they are saying about the issue, you will become so much more beneficial to them. You will provide them with a safe place to share and not vulnerable. With this type of support, you allow the person to experience emotional freedom and at their rawest without fear of rejection or discomfort from others. Learning to become a good communicator will play a large part in developing empathy in your life.

Communication

Communication in the simplest form is defined as exchanging information. This can be accomplished via talking, body language, written word, visuals and more. Today, we are going to discuss how improving communication will also improve your EQ. Often, we get caught up in trying to communicate our point or our message to others and getting frustrated when our attempts fail. We experience communication to convey our needs and wants to others, we forget that by doing so, we also make ourselves vulnerable to people sharing their needs and wants as well. A large part of our failure at communication is a lack of understanding what GOOD communication is.

Good communication is about sharing information, however, learning how to listen to what others are saying is just as important as sharing information. Now, we are talking about actively HEARING people and the messages they are trying to convey. While we want to believe we are listening to what other people are sharing, we are often distracted. We become distracted by our own thoughts, moving the conversation forward in our minds with what we will say next, or even being absorbed in something else entirely. To become an active listener, you should be able to provide a synopsis of what the other person is saying back to them at any point during the conversation.

Developing good communication is about being an active participant in the conversation so that you do not miss the subtle messages of body language, facial expressions or more. It is about not preparing your defense or thinking about the next thing you want to add to the conversation. Communication is a back and forth.

Body language can indicate a person's discomfort, anxiety or even enjoyment in the interaction. By studying and learning how to become familiar with body language you will also improve your ability to communicate. For example, when a person is upset or angry they may clench their fists, their face may become tight or they may appear to become red.

Facial expressions can also provide many clues to increase your ability to communicate with others. You can learn to recognize that someone's face may tighten up when they are upset or anxious in a situation. When people are happy or at ease they will make direct eye contact, smile, and appear more relaxed with their facial expressions.

All this knowledge can be used together to help you move towards improving your ability to communicate effectively with others. In order to improve your communication, you must learn how to put these new found skills to use.

how do you improve your communication?

To develop a better style of communication you need to become a more empathetic person, you need to figure out where you have room for improvement. Are you good at listening, but not a hearing person? Do you feel as though you spend a good part of the conversation preparing how to respond rather than actively being a part of the conversation?

If you make the commitment to improve your communication, you can try to exercise and identify what your areas of improvement are. Start by making a list of aspects of communication you weren't aware of, with that figure list in those areas, you feel comfortable improving upon. Once you decide on your list, you can move towards making the necessary improvements to your communication skills.

Wherever your potential for growth area is, you start there. Once you figure out what you need to improve upon, you slowly implement new techniques. This may include just listening to someone and not providing a response or an answer. Instead of spending your time in a conversation preparing your next statement, be active in listening to the problem. This may result in you training yourself not to interrupt another person or be ready with a response immediately. It will take time to figure out how to implement these skills into your everyday life, but the effort will be well worth it in the end.

## Chapter 3: How To Own Your Mind

One major thing that emotional intelligence does is helps you own your mind. As much as it may hurt to admit it, you may find yourself in situations where you have no say. This can happen at work, when dealing with friends or in your home life. What's more, such situations may creep up on you without notice until years go by and you start wondering why you are so unhappy with your life and where your hopes and dreams went to. You can lose control over your mind by constantly:

Accepting what you are told without bothering to question it - It's not unusual to doubt the words of strangers but what happens when you hear something from a loved one? Well, you may end up believing it simply because of the speaker. However, you need to remember that whatever story you're being told needs to be treated with a grain of salt. You need to question the story, ask for more information or clarification, do more research and make your own conclusion based on the information you have gathered. Your loved ones are human and they too get their information from somewhere else. It's easy for information to become distorted as it passes from one person to another. Thus, instead of taking what you're told as gospel truth, treat each piece of information you get objectively. This will keep your mind sharp and you will learn to see beyond biases and exaggerations.

Reacting to other people - Your emotions should not make you act in a way that is not acceptable. Words such as 'he provoked me', 'she made me angry' and so forth should not be used as an excuse to justify unacceptable behavior. You are in charge of your actions. As such, you must learn not to react but to act. The first option has a mindless ring to it. If you are reacting, you are letting your emotions get the better of you. However, when you act, you have taken the time to study the situation and determine the best way to proceed. In other words, acting takes forethought and preparation whereas reacting happens because you're driven by your emotions.

Going with the flow because doing otherwise just seems too hard - There are some things you may want to change but you don't because making that change seems like a bother. Thus, you may end up maintaining the status quo simply because you're wary of taking the steps to effect change. You may tell yourself to persevere in a bad situation because others before you did too or you will only be in the situation for a while before moving on from that place. But guess what? When you remain silent, you are sending a certain message to your brain. You're telling it that it is okay to suffer. However, you must remember that if you adopt such an attitude, you will soon find yourself enduring many stressful situations because you chose to stay silent. Little things add up in the end and they add to your unhappiness.

Not taking the time to learn about what you love - How much time do you spend on learning what you love? You may find yourself eating certain foods, watching certain TV shows, hanging out with certain people and so forth not because you love doing those things but simply because you fell into it. You should take the time to get to know yourself. If you know your likes and dislikes, you will be in a better place when it comes to spending more time on what you like and less time on things you don't like.

Not offering your opinion - Don't make a habit of dismissing people when they ask for your opinion. It may seem like a small thing to offer an opinion on what you want to eat or how a certain dress looks like or what you think of a new song. However, if you dismiss such instances or lie about your feelings, you'll create the habit of diminishing your own opinion and soon, when others do it, you'll learn to accept it and that will only lead to heartbreak.

Owning your own mind means taking charge of your emotions and your actions. You stop living a life dictated by others and start living a life that allows you to take charge and find enjoyment in things you actually like.

We have already looked at some things that you need to work on so that you can develop emotional intelligence. Let us look at some of them in light of the subject of owning your mind.

Evaluate Yourself Objectively

If you don't take an objective look at yourself, you may assume you're someone you're not. Nevertheless, the truth is the 'you' in your mind may be far from who you really are in real life. This is why you need to look at the person you've become through the years.

Start by delving into your strengths and weaknesses. Look at yourself as an observer and note down what you see. Don't just state, "I'm good at solving problems"; instead, you should follow each statement with several examples that will lead to that conclusion. As they say, doing something once does not make you an expert. You need to see where you can make improvements.

Apart from your strengths, you also need to determine your weaknesses. A weakness is something that can derail you from achieving your goals especially when you want to achieve something that requires effort. For example, if you have a weakness for junk food and you want to lose some weight, that weakness may sabotage your efforts.

However, once you know your specific weakness, you can take steps to make it a non-factor. In this case, you can get rid of junk food, create a shopping list and stick to it and stock up on healthy snacks. This way, the temptation to eat junk food will be removed altogether and this will work well towards weight loss.

After all is said and done, you want to maximize your strengths and greatly minimize your weaknesses to improve your life. This exercise is not meant to condemn you. Rather, it is meant to open your eyes to the amazing potential you have to achieve growth.

Keep a journal

Emotional intelligence has a lot to do with being aware of your thoughts and feelings. You cannot really be in control of your mind if you don't have an idea of what goes on in it. This is why you should make an effort to determine the inner workings of your mind.

One way you can track your thoughts and feelings is by keeping a journal. You should set aside a few minutes each day to go over your day and the events that occurred in that day. It would be good to note down the event, the participants, your thoughts and the feelings you had concerning that particular event or interaction.

The purpose of keeping a journal is to get a clear view of your emotions and their triggers. A journal will enable you to see whatever patterns will emerge. For example, you may discover that you become sad after watching the news and this results in you eating comfort food.

Writing your thoughts down enables you to discover a pattern of behavior that may be detrimental to your well being. Once you make the connection between your emotions and your actions, you will be in a great position to make positive changes. This is all in line with owning your mind.

Note down your priorities

Your emotions play a major role in your physical and mental wellbeing. There are things you value in your life. These things make you happy and bring you fulfillment.

If such things are constantly placed in the back burner, you'll have a hard time finding success and being happy because you'll be spending most if your time on things that you don't really care about.

Yes, it is possible to care for various things and have several goals. That is not the issue. The issue is setting your priorities to understand yourself a little better. For example, your first priority may be spending more time with your family. This does not mean that you neglect other things. Rather, it means that you will be more conscious when it comes to finding opportunities to spend time with your family.

Your goals and plans also need to be clear to you. This is because they are the road map to your future. When you have goals, you have to take steps to work towards them. These steps bring order in your life. Once you complete one-step, your mind quickly begins figuring out how to tackle the next step. You are not left constantly guessing about what to do with your day. Rather, you remain focused because your goals and priorities allow you to take charge of your mind. They direct its attention to the things you need to do and this comes in handy in fulfilling the tasks required to achieve your goals.

When you note down your goals and priorities, you build your emotional intelligence and start focusing on improving your life. You gain that control that comes with owning your mind.

Ask someone to describe you

As you've already read, it's easy to lose sight of who you are if you don't make a habit of evaluating yourself. The 'you' in your mind may be different from the 'you' other people see each day. For example, you may state that you are a kind person but when asked about the last time you performed an act of kindness, you may find it difficult to recall such a time.

In your mind, you are a kind person but your actions fail to support that claim. In this instance, your mind is filled with outdated information as it were. You need to take back your mind by updating it with new information that will help you see the 'you' you have become. This may mean asking a friend to describe you.

You can start by making a list of your qualities and comparing that list with the information your friend gives you. This way, you can adjust your list and determine which qualities to keep and which qualities you need to get rid of. The idea is to work on your strengths even as you minimize your weaknesses. If you have an intimate knowledge of who you are as a person, you will be well equipped to make the needed changes.

Practice Conscientiousness

Owning your mind means more than just being aware of your thoughts and feelings. It also means putting thought into your actions. You are not a passive observer when it comes to living your life. You are an active participant and decision maker. The actions you take have to show that you have a high emotional intelligence. This means you have to manage your emotions and express them without harming yourself. This is why you need to be conscientious.

Conscientiousness has to do with you taking responsibility for your own actions. Ultimately, you need to realize that you are responsible for the way you react when faced with certain situations. You need to be aware of your thoughts, words and actions at all times. What's more, emotional intelligence calls for you to recognize the emotions of those you are dealing with. This way, you will be able to react in a manner that won't escalate negative emotions.

Overall, in order to own your mind, you need to put emotional intelligence to good use. This means taking the time to discover who you really are and taking responsibility for your words and actions. Once you own your mind, the sky is the limit. You can do what you set out to do simply because you will have the skills you need to achieve success. But even as you work to own your mind, you also need to reduce stress. Emotional intelligence can help you with that. Let's see how this is possible.

## Chapter 4: Emotional Intelligence, and the Environments of Daily Life

Home and Personal

Your everyday relationships with your significant other, children, relatives and close friends are directly affected by your level of emotional intelligence. Outside of work, this is the area if your life where you will spend the most time relating to others.

When an emergency occurs, it is those individuals with the most stable emotions that take charge and help while others are set into a panic. Such people can remain calm while other come unhinged. When the ones you love are trapped in an emotional bubble of any kind, you can be a beacon of light that lends calm and a level-headed approach to whatever is happening.

Moreover, then, armed with clearer insight, you can alter your perception to the situation, and help others to see things differently and find solutions that they may have never seen in the cloudy haze of emotions.

Work and Career

Population statistics suggest that most people will spend nearly 60% of their waking lives in the workplace. Whether you are giving orders or taking orders, emotional intelligence and a peace of mind in the career environment is a must have. When we think about how much time is spent with fellow employees and managers while looming over a desk, it makes no sense to spend thousands of hours of your life in a state of stress. Some have even fooled themselves into thinking that higher stress and pent up emotions is just something that comes with the territory at work, but it does not have to be.

Developing emotional intelligence when dealing with fellow employees, supervisors, and clients are essential for harmonious interactions at work. Those who have high EI are often favored, admired, and granted more promotions because they know how to relate well to the chain of command at work. They can perceive the best opportunities or action by observing the emotions of their superiors, and respond accordingly.

Schools

It is far harder to learn anything or even to concentrate if your emotions are not in check. Many students who find it difficult to remember Concepts or acquire new things often have issues with dealing with their feelings and concentration. Often when one cannot fully concentrate, his or her emotions are affecting them in some way.

The heart of any distraction is usually a focus on some event or idea, but its presence in your consciousness directly affects your ability to complete something else. Feeling anxiety in the classroom or playing out stressful imaginary sequences in your head does not help. On the other hand, some people feel so restless that they cannot sit still long enough in any learning environment. If you can put aside distracting emotions that arise from thinking about other topics, you will find it much easier to study, take full advantage of the learning environment and absorb more knowledge instead of wallowing in unwanted emotions and thoughts.

Public and Social Life

Many people are deeply admired for their ability to get along well with others. Having emotional intelligence can help you get very far with building relationships with anyone. Whether you are building stronger relationships with your family, loved one's, associates, or your neighbors, having higher emotional intelligence can make each one of those interactions more fruitful.


Many act on their emotions no matter the consequences, while others can keep their cool and respond effectively to all kinds of situations. If you look closely, you will see that emotions have the capacity to influence the entire world through people. With this realization, it makes sense for everyone to develop their emotional intelligence to make the most of his or her existence and live a more joyful life.

## Chapter 5: The Building Blocks of Emotional Intelligence

In the previous chapter, we discussed the importance of self-awareness, but let's talk about some strategies for implementing it, as well as the other stepping stones of becoming more emotionally intelligent. Everything is a process, and emotional intelligence is no different.

Self-Awareness

Gaining control over your stress levels is just the first building block of emotional intelligence. The science behind attachment shows that your current emotional environment is likely a reflection of what happened when you were a child. Your capability to manage your core emotions pertaining to sadness, anger, fear, and happiness depends on the consistency and quality of your early life's

41

emotional environment. As a baby, if your primary caregiver valued and understood your feelings, it's likely that your feelings are a valuable asset in your adult life. However, if your emotional experiences as a baby were threatening, confusing, or downright painful, then it's likely you've attempted to distance yourself from what you're really feeling.

However, being able to feel your emotions, having a constant connection with what you're feeling, is the imperative factor to understanding how your emotions influence your actions and thoughts.

Let's take a look at some circumstances that should be truths for you in your life. If any of these experiences are not familiar to you, then your emotions might be 'turned off.' To build your emotional intelligence, you must first reconnect with your core emotions, accept your feelings, and become comfortable with those feelings.

Are you someone who encounters one emotion after another as your environment changes from moment to moment? Do your emotions flow?

Are your emotions expressed with physical sensations that you experience in areas like your throat, stomach, or chest?

Do you experience a single emotion or feeling, such as sadness, anger, joy, or fear, that are obvious in restrained facial expressions?

Do your emotions factor into the decisions you make? Are you paying attention to your feelings?

One way to become more in tune with your emotions and how they are affecting you is to practice mindfulness. Mindfulness is the practice of focusing your attention on the current moment purposefully without judgement. Most religions have some sort of meditation technique or prayer technique that is similar to meditation, but it can be an agnostic practice. To begin practicing mindfulness in order to become in tune with your emotions, follow these steps.

Take a couple of minutes to focus on your breathing. Don't control it but just focus on it.

Notice how you're currently feeling. Are you feeling good, bad, happy, sad, pleasant, or unpleasant?

What word is best for describing the emotion you're feeling?

Maintain your attention on that emotion's intensity, your breathing, your posture, and what else you're feeling in your body.

Notice the thoughts and judgments you're having. You may want to cling to the positive emotions and let go of the negative one, but just notice your thoughts with considering them to be either positive or negative.

If other emotions come about, notice what feeling has come into your thoughts. Describe as you did in step two and three.

After you're finished, take a moment to reflect on how you may hold onto or reject certain feelings.

Self-Management

In order for you to employ your emotional intelligence, you have to be able to use your feelings to make good decisions about your behavior. When you're overly stressed out, you might lose control of your emotions and the capability to act appropriately and thoughtfully.

Think back to a moment when you were overwhelmed by stress. Was it easy for you to make a rational decision and think clearly? Most likely, it wasn't. When you were stressed, your capability to think rationally and clearly became compromised.

Emotions are an important piece of information that tell you about yourself and those around you, but in the face of stress that removes you from your comfort zone, you can become overwhelmed and lose your sense of self. When you're able to manage stress and stay present emotionally, you learn to receive information that might be negative without losing your self-control. You can make choices that will allow you to control impulsive behaviors and emotions, manage your emotions healthily, take initiatives, adapt to changing circumstances, and follow through on your commitments.

One way to immediately reduce your stress levels is to breathe through your nose slowly, without opening your mouth to exhale. Feel the air filling your lungs, and then release it slowly and gently. This is a good way to buy yourself a little time to think about what you're going to say or do before you say or do it.

Social Awareness

The third building block for emotional intelligence is being aware of others' emotions. Social awareness lets you recognize and figure out the nonverbal cues others are always using to communicate with you. These cues will let you know how someone is really feeling, how their emotional state is from moment to moment, and what's important to them. When a group of people send out a similar nonverbal cue, you're able to understand the power of dynamics and read them better. In short, you're socially comfortable and empathetic.

This is another area where mindfulness can really help. To build social awareness, you must recognize the importance of mindfulness in the social process. You're not able to notice the refined, nonverbal cues when you're constantly thinking about yourself, thinking about something else, or just zoning out altogether. Social awareness requires that you are present in the moment. While many people are proud to be able to multitask, doing so means you're missing the subtle emotional cues taking place in others that will help you understand them better.

Set aside your thoughts and focus on the interaction that is happening. You're more likely to further your social goals this way.

Follow the flow of others emotional responses, and pay attention to yours, too.

Pay attention to others, but know that it's not diminishing your self-awareness either. When you invest effort and time into paying attention to others, you gain an insight into your personal emotional state, as well as your beliefs and values. For example, if you feel upset by someone else's views, you've learned something important about yourself.

Relationship Awareness

The final building block is relationship awareness. Working well with your peers, spouse, friends, family members, and strangers is a process that starts with emotional awareness and your capability to recognize and comprehend what others are experiencing. Once emotional awareness is happening, you can develop additional emotional and social skills that will help your relationships grow.

Here are three ways you can become more emotionally aware in relationships.

#1 Become aware of how you use nonverbal communication.

It's not possible to avoid sending nonverbal cues to those around you about what you're thinking and feeling. The numerous muscles in your face, especially the ones around your mouth, eyes, nose, and forehead, help you wordlessly convey your emotions, as well as read the emotional intent of others. The emotional part of the brain is always working; even if you choose to ignore its messages, others aren't going to. Recognizing nonverbal cues that you send to those around you can play an integral part in improving your relationships.

#2 Use laughter to relieve stress.

Laughter and humor are natural stress relievers. They loosen you up and help relieve your burdens while still keeping everything in perspective. Laughter will bring your nervous system into an equilibrium, reducing your stress, calming you, sharpening your wits, and making you empathetic toward yourself and others.

#3 Learn to see conflicts as an opportunity to grow closer to someone.

Arguments and disagreements are inevitable in any relationship. Two people are never going to have the exact same needs, expectations, and opinions all the time. However, that doesn't have to be a bad thing. Resolving conflict in a healthy manner can strengthen the bond between two people. When conflict is not seen as being punishment or threatening, it helps grow creativity, freedom, and safety in a relationship.

Now that you're aware of the building blocks of emotional intelligence, let's move on to discovering what emotions you're feeling, as well as how to read others' emotional cues.

## Chapter 6: Improving your emotional intelligence

The first step is self-perception. This is crucial. You cannot skip this step. You may think that you know yourself deep down inside. You may think that you are a very self-aware person. Guess what? Think again.

In many cases, we assume that our emotions. We make all sorts of snap judgments about how we feel. Little do we know that we're actually feeling many things at the same time. This always shocks people, even those who claim to be totally self-aware. This is why at this point in time, I need you to drop all your assumptions about how well you know yourself.

Instead, ask yourself a very simple question, "How aware am I of all my emotional states?" Pay attention to the word "all." This is plural. Every time you feel strong emotions, it usually doesn't just involve one emotion. You're feeling something before, during and after that strong emotional state. If you ignore this or dismiss it outright, you're doing yourself a big disservice. You really are.

You're putting yourself in a situation where there's a disconnect between how you're feeling and how others perceive you. You have to understand that there is often a disconnect between what you think you feel and what others say you're feeling. Now, this is not a question of opposition. This is not a question of black and white opposites, that either one is true and the other one is false.

Instead, this is a question of seeing the big picture. For example, you're feeling depressed that your ex-girlfriend is going out with somebody else. But if you dig deep enough, you're not just feeling sadness. You're also feeling nostalgia and a sense of disappointment in yourself because you did not treat her better. You may even be feeling angry at yourself.

There are so many different emotions that are going on. It's kind of like a tossed salad. There are many different layers to this emotional state that you're in. It would help tremendously if you consult with other people to get the view from outside. You may feel just totally depressed, but it may well turn out that there are other things going on.

If you aware of these and you are able to overcome your own sense of denial, then you become less disconnected. You will be able to clearly express your emotions better, but most importantly, you will become more aware of what you are truly feeling in any point in time.

The problem of denial

Why do people play the denial game? Why do people lie to themselves? Well, a part of that is due to the fact that we are playing to the crowd. For example, guys are not supposed to feel sad. You're supposed to be tough, independent and autonomous. Negative feelings should slide off you like water off a duck's back.

Similarly, if you're a female, you're supposed to feel empathetic. You're supposed to be compassionate. So, when you feel contempt and anger, you get confused. You have to overcome this and replace it with a deep sense of authenticity.

You have to remember that there is no such thing as a right and wrong emotion. What's important is that you are fully aware that you are feeling it. That's all you need to do. Acknowledge that you are feeling it. Clearly identify it. There is nothing to explain. There is nothing to be embarrassed about. There is nothing to sweep under the rug. Just acknowledge it.

Don't label it as ugly, inappropriate or something a "bad person" would feel. Your job is to be as clear as possible about the emotions that you're feeling. Take ownership of them. There's no need to apologize for them. Overcome this natural sense of denial because since we were children, we were trained to deny our feelings. We were trained to make excuses for them. Well, starting now, you're going to have to overcome that.

You can't assume that you'll automatically be understood

Another problem that gets in the way of a heightened level of emotional self-perception is the idea that people will automatically "get us." I really can't blame people for thinking this way. After all, when you were a kid and you were going through your emotional growing pains, your parents gave you a lot of rope and they played along. They may have even enabled you.

The problem is, at some point, you're going to have to grow up. The people around you are not going to bend over backwards to try to understand you. They're not going to give you the benefit of the doubt. They definitely are not going to give you much rope. Don't put yourself in the position of constantly assuming that people will automatically understand what you're expressing and what your words truly mean.

You have to understand that people have enough problems of their own. They have their own lives to live. Otherwise, you're putting yourself in the situation where people are basically going to be walking on eggshells around you. You will be a very unpleasant person to be around. You don't want to play that game.

You have to get rid of this mental crutch. The more you believe that people will automatically understand what you're feeling, the less likely you're going to be doing the heavy emotional work of being truly emotionally self-aware.

Stop playing to the crowd

In addition to what I described above. Another way people play to the crowd involves some sort of emotional "Kabuki Theater." Have you seen a Kabuki show? The emotions of the actors fixed. They are formulaic. It doesn't take a rocket scientist or a very sensitive person to figure them out. In fact, you can actually read people's emotions in Kabuki because they are very easy to tell apart.

When you play to the crowd, you are engaged in Kabuki Theater. on an emotional level. Why? Well, when you express your emotions based on social expectations, you're not really showing your real face. You're not really expressing what you truly feel. Instead, you look at your situation and imagine what the "right" emotional state is.

In other words, you're looking for what's socially acceptable. Then you express your emotions along those lines, exactly like Kabuki Theater. Life does not work on formulas. Unfortunately, the more you do this and play to the crowd this way, the less emotionally honest you become. Eventually, you reach a point where you can't even tell your own emotions unless they are reduced to cartoonish simplification.

Stop playing to the crowd emotionally. Don't let social expectations dictate how you express yourself emotionally.

Focus on honesty

If you're feeling sad, feel sad. If you're feeling upset, feel upset. Now, please understand that this doesn't mean lashing out. This doesn't mean that you have to bawl your eyes out or yell at somebody in anger. I'm talking about what you're feeling deep down inside. Instead of covering it up, pretending it's something else or, worse yet, denying it, feel it.

Honesty is its own reward. If you keep covering up what you're feeling, the only person you're fooling is yourself. Remember, emotions have two levels. There is the purely subjective emotion and you're the only person who can feel this, but there is also the external part. When you manifest emotions, other people can see signals that you're sending out.

Unfortunately, unless you are completely honest with what you're feeling, oftentimes, there is a disconnect between the objective signals you're sending out and what you subjectively feel. This type of honesty is its own reward. The more you practice honesty deep down inside, the better off you will become.

Log your emotions

Keep an emotional intelligence journal. Your first step is to log your emotions. Once you're clear, you're going to have to overcome denial and stop playing to the crowd. Log what you're feeling. Remember, there is no right or wrong answer. Nobody has to read your notes. It's not like you're going to write all this down and post it on Facebook. This is for your eyes only.

Just write whatever is at the top of your head. This is the subjective part. As long as you feel it, write it down. Next, describe it in objective terms. This is very important. What is the context of your feelings? What brought it on? What exactly do you feel?

For example, if the mental image of my ex-girlfriend who cheated on me flashed in my mind, I would write, I feel sad because she betrayed me. She didn't tell the truth. She told me lie after lie to my face. She let me go on, knowing full well that she was doing certain things behind my back. It was only until I discovered that she was doing these things, that she told me the truth. This is why I feel bad.

When you write along these lines, you're being objective because you are tracing what you feel, which is sadness, to a set of facts that happened in a specific time and a specific place in your personal history. This is the objective portion of your log. You're creating context when you do this.

Now, the next part is subjective. You ask yourself, what do I think I'm feeling? I think I'm feeling sadness, but is there anything else? I feel nostalgia because I truly loved her. I believed her. A part of me would like to think that she loved me too. She seemed conflicted at the end when we broke up.

After you've written this type of material, you ask yourself, what are the objective factors here? What are the things that I can test? Well, you can test the fact that she lied to you because you talked to your common friends and they told you the truth. You can test the fact that she did all these things.

In that context, it's okay to feel sad and that's what you're really feeling. You're also feeling angry and betrayed. You're feeling abandoned. The key here is to list down all the emotions that would be warranted by the facts. That's how you get to your real emotions. You can't just say, I feel sad," or "I feel angry," or, "I feel regretful." That is too shallow.

You have to look at the whole set of facts, pay attention to the context and then list down all the emotions that could possibly come. After that, ask yourself, "Am I feeling this?" That's how you break down that iceberg of emotions, instead of just vainly scraping the surface.

If you keep going through this process, you start seeing the big picture of how your emotions stack up and how you express them.

Ask a friend

When you're interacting with your friends like telling jokes, hearing sad stories, listening to them and just basically hanging out together, stop and ask them, "Look at my face. Pay attention to my words. Look at how I'm carrying myself. What do you think I am feeling?"

Now, please understand that you have to do this with real friends because real friends care. But there is also a chance that they will try to give you the answer that you're looking for because they don't want to offend you. They want to remain your friends. You have to give them permission to be completely honest.

Ask your friend what he or she perceives based on facts. This is the most important part. They have to tell you their interpretation of your feelings, but they have to give facts to support it. Maybe they would say, "Yeah, I saw you smirking, so I think that you were upset when we were talking about your ex-girlfriend. I saw you with a smile in your eyes when you're talking about Jennifer. Maybe you really enjoyed being friends with that classmate of yours," and so on and so forth.

The key here is to get them to say facts. Remember, it's not going to help you if your friend just says, "Well, I think you're still feeling guilty about what you did to Eduardo 20 years ago." That doesn't help because it's purely subjective. Who knows how they came up with that conclusion? So, ask for facts.

What you're doing is you're trying to correlate what you're subjectively feeling with what your friend perceives objectively. This goes a long way in fixing that disconnect that I described earlier.

Train yourself

Now that you have logged your emotions and asked friends, you should have enough information regarding whatever disconnect may exist between your subjective feelings and how you externalize or communicate these feelings. At the very least, you would be more aware of the emotional signals that you are sending out.

Armed with this information, you can ask yourself what the objective parameters are of certain emotions. What kind of emotional range do I normally exhibit when I'm feeling these certain types of strong emotions: sadness, happiness, joy, anger, shock, guilt, regret, etc.

Remember, strong emotions often happen within a range. It's not just one emotion that you're feeling. Now that you have a fairly clear understanding of your range of emotions and the objective parameters for those, what they're supposed to look like and how you communicate them, the next step is to train yourself to emote in objectively clear terms.

It's very important to then look at the range of emotions and be as clear about them as you can. This way, when you feel sad, people perceive that you are sad. Not shocked, not nostalgic, not guilty, but sad. If you're upset and angry, that's what people should perceive you as. You have to train yourself on two levels.

You have to learn how to emote the emotions that you're feeling in clear terms objectively, so people are less likely to misread you. This, of course, assumes that you learned an earlier lesson, which is that you are fully in tune with what you're feeling. You're not mislabeling it, you're not in denial, nor are you taking one emotion over another.

Instead, you are fully aware of what you're feeling at all times. This takes a lot of work because, let's face it, most people are lazy. Most people would rather make assumptions of strong emotions that they feel and leave it at that. This emotional self-awareness is the foundation of emotional control. Get this right and you are well on your way to self-mastery, create your personal success and higher emotional intelligence.

## Chapter 7: Conflict Management

So far, you have learned to how to separate your emotions from your logic and how to empathize with others. Both of these solutions only take us so far. We now need to look at ways in which we can put those skills together and use them to manage conflict. Conflict management is a critical ability to have, especially in a workplace scenario. Our ability to manage it is one of the most important assets in good leadership.

●Re-assess your position. Before diving in and presenting your suggestion for a way forward, take a few moments to consider whether, after all the new information offered, your position remains the same. In the face of new information, it is only sensible to re-evaluate. That does not mean that you are wrong or that you are going to have to change course, but it does mean that you are considering all possible options. If you need more time to weigh up the new information and opinions then say so and take that time. It will buy you more respect that bulldozing your way forward without reflecting.

●Be results driven. In any environment, conflict will appear at certain stages. It is part of the human condition. The important thing to recognize is that not all conflict is bad and that, when managed correctly, conflict can increase creativity and productivity. That is why we look at this from the point of view of management rather than just resolution. When conflict arises, you now have the necessary skills to observe clinically, and unemotionally, and at the same time have begun to develop your levels of sensitivity to a point where you can empathize with others. It is at the point where you have understood all of the conflicting opinions that you need to start trying to influence the outcome. That outcome will be based around the results that you now consider most appropriate.

Having understood all of the points on offer, you may or may not have moved your own opinion, but you must now have a clear idea of the result that you wish to achieve. Don't underestimate the importance of this step or you will be wishy washy in your responses. People need to see you acting from a position of strength and with a clear idea of where you are going. They may have their own ideas that differ from yours, but if you act with confidence and focus you are in a strong position to get the outcome you want. Remember, you fully understand their position, whereas they probably don't fully understand yours.

●Seek collaborative solutions. As you fully understand all sides to the argument you are in an ideal position to state your goals but in a way that includes as much of the conflicting position as is sensible. We are not right all of the time and we must train ourselves to see where there is an overlap in our position, and also which parts of another person's position are valid to the result we desire. If someone else has offered an opinion that is pertinent, don't reject it out of sheer stubbornness. Rather, try to find a way to incorporate it into your own solution. Give credit where credit is due and mention that that part of the plan is from someone else. This will cement their support for your case more strongly.

●State your case clearly. In order to achieve your result and avoid further conflict, the way you talk at this stage is going to be important. State clearly the result you are pursuing but also recap the position that others have suggested so that it is obvious that you have taken their point of view into consideration. Most people, when they know that their opinions have been sympathetically considered, will back down when confronted with another logical viewpoint. If you have presented your case calmly and logically and demonstrated that you understand the conflicting opinions thoroughly, there are only three ways things can go. One is that they will accept your position because it is obviously better. The second is that they will accept your position because it is at least as good as their own but you have expressed it better. The third scenario is that they dig in their heels simply because they have not developed their own emotional intelligence to a point where they are able to walk away from a difference of opinion without getting their own way.

•Dealing with the stubborn. If you are forced to confront someone who has allowed their emotional position to overrule their logic, you need to be very careful. One way of doing this is by sticking to questions and statements of fact. Undeniable facts are difficult to object to. They are the worst enemy of the emotionally dogmatic because they expose that person's dogma and lack of logic. These sorts of people are often very poor at emotional intelligence, but they are also sometimes the loudest and most opinionated. Quietly confronting them with facts that cannot be refuted sometimes, but not always, disarms them.

●Be prepared to walk away. It is not a good idea to corner someone who is not prepared to let logic dominate their thought processes, especially in a group environment. Instead, after logically and calmly expressing yourself through stated facts and questions, step back from the possible confrontation. In a group environment your logic will have been witnessed and you will not strengthen your case by getting baited into an argument that you have already won. Suggest a timeout and hope that common sense will reassert itself when the other person has cooled down or let others take over the argument and do the persuading for you. In the end, what you are looking for is a win-win scenario and that Holy

Grail may not be achieved on the first attempt.

●You don't win every battle. After working hard at your emotional intelligence, it can be hard to accept that you won't always get your own way, even when logic tells you that you are right and you have used all of the skills in this book. Consider that losing battles gracefully is part and parcel of a broader war and that you are building a base that will stand you in good stead over the long term. What you are in the process of doing is establishing yourself as an emotionally stable and clear thinking individual. Part of this includes recognizing that emotional intelligence is a matter of growth and that from time to time you will be forced to give way to situations that are neither logical nor intelligent. You need to have enough faith in your new abilities to know that they will overcome in the end.

## Chapter 8: Relaxation Activities

Individuals with depression frequently battle with more passionate weight than discouragement alone. Melancholy and uneasiness frequently go as one, and anxiety can likewise challenge your passionate wellbeing.

At the point when tension and anxiety develop, they can influence your sorrow side effects and make them harder to oversee. Some simple relaxation techniques may help you get away from your anxiety and uneasiness, and also better deal with your feeling of the depression.

How Relaxation Helps Depression

Nurturing all parts of your emotional well-being is vital for managing sadness, and that implies facilitating anxiety and uneasiness, as well. An every-day measurement of relaxation may be simply what the specialist requested.

Tension, which is normal in individuals who have sadness, can make individuals feel strained. The uneasiness can be serious, says Dr. Payne, and may even prompt frenzy assaults.

"Absolutely when somebody is depressed, much of their thinking process is negative," includes Payne. "Relaxation methods can help with that; it can cut individuals down an indent so that they're not all that on edge or negative.

"Relaxation techniques, for instance, meditation, massage, and mild breathing exercises can likewise release endorphins, which are chemicals in the body that ease torment and are thought to lift your temperament.

Relaxation also benefits your physical wellbeing. "It's an alternate instrument to fight those physical impacts of depression," Payne (Psychologist in U.S.) says.

Relaxation strategies may even help counteract depression in some individuals. As indicated by Payne, "Natural anxiety can trigger depressive scenes, so if you have a hereditary inclination to sorrow, and you experience an unpleasant time, you are more inclined to have a depressive scene. Figuring out how to control your anxiety levels may help forestall depressive scenes."

Relaxation Techniques for Depression

Which relaxation exercises will be best for enhancing emotional well-being relies on upon the individual, says Payne. Some individuals discover a massage or pedicure to be cooling, while those exercises could really cause stress for somebody who doesn't delight in them. Your relaxation method doesn't need to be confounded; anything that makes you loosen up and feel great will benefit your emotional well-being.

Here are some relaxation methods known to help ease gloom and tension. Attempt the ones that speak to you, and find which ones convey the most push easing.

Profound Relaxing- Profound, moderate breathing can help you release nervousness and relax from head to toe. Attempt it at set times for the duration of the day or at whatever point you feel anxiety building. Consolidate profound breathing with meditation for considerably more prominent relaxing, anxiety easing, and centering.

Mild Exercise- This is an extraordinary relaxation strategy, says Payne, and it offers incredible physical well-being benefits, as well. Yoga is an especially gainful help on the grounds that it concentrates on meditation, parity, profound breathing, and relaxing all in the meantime.

Surround your-self with Aromas- Some individuals find certain charming fragrances exceptionally relaxing. Known as fragrance based treatment, this method can be as simple as lighting a candle scented with a most loved scent.

Take a get-away in your mind- Called visual or guided symbolism, this relaxation procedure uses your creative energy to divert yourself from every day stress. Envision yourself in a peaceful, quiet place that makes you upbeat. Require some time to experience all the sensations in your mind.

Warm up- Treat yourself to a long, extravagant absorb an air pocket shower or lose yourself in the steam of a hot shower. Actually tasting on a mug of hot espresso coffee, tea, or cocoa can be calming.

Scrawl out your anxiety- In the event that something's disturbing you and you simply need to move it out into the open, a journal or diary can be your closest companion. Take a couple of minutes every day or at whatever time you feel down or focused on to expound on your reasons for alarm, concerns, or disappointments.

Everybody's concept of relaxation is distinctive. It doesn't make a difference what you do to diminish stretch the length of it helps you feel better. Set aside a few minutes every day for a short reprieve, something that you anticipate and that will abandon you feeling more cheerful as you face whatever is left of the day.

Relaxation Mild Exercise

Keep in mind, relaxation doesn't mean you are "doing nothing" or simply being languid. We all need eventually to ourselves. You ought to consider unwinding a vital need of life, such as consuming or dozing. It's a key to staying great.

For each of the relaxation activities mentioned, it is suggested that you find a decent, calm place where you know you won't be exasperates for the span of the activity.

Make arrange an agreeable seat that will allow you to sit up straight using good posture. How you sit in your seat is essential for greatest benefit. Be comfortable the little of your once again to the back of the seat and sit upright.

This will allow you to take long smooth breaths, and your lungs to completely expand with oxygen. Don't hold your arms or legs, yet sit with your legs at a ninety degree pose. Rest your arms comfortably in your lap without using armrests. If you utilize armrests, this may prompt muscle pressure in your shoulders, neck and back.

Some people like to close their eyes amid these relaxation activities. If you don't wish to close your eyes, you may find a settled point in the room and let your look center upon it. Postpone the activity if you experience physical or emotional distress.

You may attempt each of the relaxation activities as suggested. Some people observe that they incline toward one or two more than the others. When you find which one you like, it is suggested that you hone them consistently so you can assemble the aptitude and make the practice more viable for you.

It is suggested that you begin with the "Diaphragmatic Breathing" as this is an essential presentation for optional activities.

# Chapter 9: Experiencing Silence

Have you ever thought about why people meditate or why they try mindfulness in their lives? Both of these are huge in this day and age and for a good reason. We are invaded by noise and influence all of the time and sometimes, you need to turn that influence off and merely look inward. Mindfulness helps you to retain very little bias, and meditation clears out the cobwebs of the mind so that you are not restricting yourself mentally and are letting your subconscious mind have the silence that it needs.

The way that the mind works is that you consciously think things and associate them and link them in such a way that a single thought becomes a pattern of ideas. Meditation teaches you to concentrate on one idea – that of breathing – and to try to remain neutral when it comes to the thoughts that invade your mind during the course of meditation. It's not really about physical effort or even mental effort because if you try too hard, you can't meditate. Meditation is more of a flow that comes over you when you silence the mind and concentrate on your breathing.

One of the hardest lessons I can teach students is to silence the mind. They try too hard, when in fact all they have to do is acknowledge the thought and then let go of it, without allowing the chain of thoughts to form. If you try too hard at doing this, you form other equally destructive thought patterns, which may consist of you telling yourself off for having thoughts in the first place. Letting go sounds simple but it isn't at all simple and requires daily practice to work automatically, but it happens in all different areas of your life that you may not be aware of at this moment in time. Think of the things that you do every day on autopilot.

Meditation is a little like those things because you are not actually thinking about it. You are merely doing it. As it gets to be a habit, you will do that on autopilot as well, which is why meditation instructors tell you to set a certain amount of time aside for meditation on a daily or twice daily basis.

Emotionally intelligent people notice things that other people don't notice. We all have the ability to use what we call intuition, though, with all of the noise of the world, people have forgotten how to trust their gut instincts. I read a book the other week that was telling the story of a young woman who was raped in her own home. When she was questioned by a police officer doing a study on intuition, all the signs that she was in danger were in place, but because of her busy head and lifestyle, she ignored them. Emotionally intelligent people don't do that. They permit their instincts to guide them, and that's basically what they are there for.

The body is good at protecting itself, though if the mind does not hear the messages being sent to it, what good are they? Thus, if you can find that quiet place each day to meditate, it's a good idea because it helps your breathing, the oxygen distribution in your body and also helps to quieten the thoughts that may be blocking intuition out.

Controlling your thoughts

Let's take an instance in anyone's life and show you how thoughts are controlled. Someone who allows emotions to rule will see something in an entirely different way to a person who is in control of his thoughts and feelings. Let's try and imagine for a moment that you have three people who witness the same thing. A bird swoops down and lands on their heads.

1)One person will see this as a threat and will panic.

2)One person will just move his head so that the bird flies away.

3)One person will conjure up all kinds of potential scenarios that may happen as a consequence of the bird landing on his/her head.

Which do you believe is the emotionally intelligent answer? The second one is the answer that people should use if they have their wits about them and are realistic about the situation. The other alternatives attach emotions and perhaps associations that don't need to be attached to the situation and make the moment harder for themselves.

If you put aside ten minutes in the morning and ten minutes in the evening and do as I show you below, you will find yourself more likely to pause and take stock of situations before panicking and before making those situations more significant than they really are:

●Sit on a chair and breathe into the count of 8 making sure your back is straight and your feet level on the floor.

●Breathe out to the count of ten.

●Do it again and realize that meditation is simply doing this and thinking about nothing else at all.

●Carry on breathing in this way, dismissing thoughts as they happen and carrying on with the breathing. Think of the thoughts like balloons and just let them go.

This exercise will slow down your heartbeat and your blood pressure but more than that, it will allow your mind the silence that you need. It is best to do this first thing in the morning and again before you eat your evening meal. You should be in a place, which doesn't distract your mind. You can also use this method to clear your mind before important events in your life. Let the mind experience silence, and you get to be able to control how your emotions jump in during your day to day activities. You pause and then react, and this silence of the mind will enable you to react in a much more emotionally intelligent way.

# CHAPTER 10: TURNING TOWARD THE POSITIVE

I have talked a lot so far about resetting our minds. In fact, that may be the wrong expression to use as it implies that we set our minds in the first place, which most of us did not do on our own. Instead of intentionally developing our thinking processes we mainly just acquire a set of reactions to the various circumstances we encounter as we go about our daily lives. How we react to those circumstances and events is often not thought through and our responses may be more instinctive than considered. The problem comes when we hang on more to the negative thought and reaction processes, which as I have already pointed out, are the most common way in which humans deal with things. Many of us pay more attention to what we put into our cereal bowls in the morning than what we put into our minds during the course of our days. Of course there are also people whose mental outlook has been conditioned by traumatic incidents that may have taken place many years earlier.

Either way we seem to somehow allow the negative to drown out the positive. In order to begin to think positively we need to reverse that process. This may not be easy at first, as our minds will constantly throw negative thoughts at us, as this is its natural default mechanism. The first thing we need to get in the habit of doing is examining our thoughts and differentiating between the positive and the negative. This can be quite an enlightening process as we suddenly discover, often to our surprise, how many of our thoughts are negative. Initially you will probably be assaulted with thoughts telling you how pointless it is to try to change your thinking. After that, as our minds slump back into their comfortably familiar negative zone we start to see how they function when left to their own devices. I frequently find myself having mental arguments with people, shop assistants, employers etc. with whom I am about to have a meeting. My mind will run through every negative scenario possible and how I should aggressively overcome those conflicts that I have created in my mind. Of course, in almost every case the conflict never takes place. It was purely a defense mechanism that my mind puts itself through to be prepared just in case the worst should happen. As you will discover the invention of disaster scenarios is one of the negative thinker's greatest abilities.

Once we have shocked ourselves with the many negative thoughts we manage to create and learned to identify them we can embark on a process of counter attack. We need to learn to stop negative thoughts in their tracks. It is not easy, however, to simply wipe out a negative thought. Our mind will simply replace it with another thought and as there is such an abundant supply of negativity to draw on the chances are that thought too will have negative connotations. Instead we need to replace it with a positive one. The goal here is not just to drown out negative thinking but also to make positive thinking the default position that your minds drops into when left unattended. I am not suggesting that this will be easy but with a little discipline it will happen and the rewards you reap in terms of peace of mind will be invaluable. Little by little we will be able to recognize when negative thoughts are beginning to occur and then be able to replace them with their positive opposition.

You will need to learn to recognize the situations that trigger negative thinking and to take measures to avoid those situations or start thinking positively before the poor quality thoughts can develop. One common situation that triggers negativity that I face is whilst driving in heavy traffic. Driving is the one condition where I can be sure that everyone in front of me is an idiot and everyone behind me a moron. Of course when trapped in negative mode the possibility that I may even think that somebody is a moron or idiot does not even occur to me. One only has to look at the way some people behave in heavy traffic to know how stress provoking it can be. We can't all avoid driving but if we are aware that it perverts our calm thinking then we are already in a good position to maintain calm minds. Once we have accepted that some of the people out there are going to drive like idiots and there is nothing we can do about it we can relax and just accept that though we cannot control the traffic we can control how we will react to it. Some deep breathing, a little nice music and a bit of focus on anything good that may have happened during your day and suddenly that commute is not quite as bad as you thought it was, especially if you surrender to the fact that, regardless of how you think, you are not going to get there any faster than the conditions allow.

Moving beyond just offering counter thoughts is the next step. We need to start speaking positively as well. When we are in company the conversation will almost always veer toward the negative at some stage. People will begin to complain about something or someone. This is because, like the old negative person that you used to be, the people you are talking to have minds that are filled with negative thoughts. The new person you are in the process of building needs to bring positivity to the conversation. It is not as difficult as it sounds. When someone offers an opinion that is negative you simply turn the argument on its head and offer a positive viewpoint. You don't need to be controversial or combative; you just need to find something positive to say.

People who were accustomed to the more pessimistic and cynical character you used to be will be a little surprised when you first exit the closet with your mind neatly dressed in its new positive outfit, but they will adapt; if they don't then move on.

This brings me neatly to my next point. Try not to surround yourself with negative thinking people. Positivity feeds on positivity. Negative people just suck away your energy and lead you back into your old ways. When possible avoid them altogether and when you can't then be sure to cling even more tightly to your positive mindset. We are easily influenced by those around us. It is a natural human reaction to want to fit in and to be part of a group that often requires agreeing with the way they think and talk. This very normal behavior means that when negative comments are expressed they soon become amplified by people concurring. To offer a comment that flies in the face of such unity takes a little courage at first and may feel somewhat provocative as most of us are conditioned to go with the crowd rather than against it. What often happens in reality is that others pick up on the positivity and the whole tide of the conversation can suddenly be turned. I believe that this is because, very often, most of the negativity being expressed is not necessarily deeply felt but has just become the fall back position taken by people with a negative mindset when having any conversation. The offering of a more positive viewpoint may well be picked up quite readily.

In our negative mindset we became adept at catastrophizing things in our minds. We could blow up the most innocuous of forthcoming events and turn it into a looming disaster. This is not surprising given the world we live in. If it were not for looming disasters I believe most of the press would go out of business. Sometimes it is helpful to look back at how many of those earthshaking, cataclysmic events never took place. In 1999 we were suddenly inundated with reports that at the stroke of midnight on the 31$^{st}$ of December every computer on the planet was going to suddenly stop working which would hurl us toward an Armageddon like fate. Looking back in hindsight the whole drama now seems laughable. Now take a look at some of the problems you anticipated recently in your own life that either never materialized at all or which turned out to be far less catastrophic than you had thought they would be. As you learn to examine your thoughts you will see this as a behavioral process we exhibit frequently if we don't discipline ourselves to think more positively.

For some people personalizing is a big problem. They see any problem that occurs to be the result of their own behavior or some inadequacy in the way they behave. This negative form of self-perception often started somewhere in their childhood and has been carried with them for many years. It is a dangerous mental process to hang on to because in some ways it becomes self-fulfilling. If a person constantly tells himself or herself "Oh I could never stand up and talk in front of an audience" then the probability that they will fail when called upon to do so are much higher. People with such a poor self-esteem are very vulnerable to negative thoughts and yet they are the very people that would benefit the most from a change in thinking.

While there are some people for whom this thinking process is deeply entrenched we all have some areas of our lives in which we perceive ourselves to be weak and less likely to succeed. So powerful is the influence of the mind that it is most unlikely that we would become competent in these vulnerable zones unless we first identify them and replace the negative thoughts with positive ones. Forced positive thinking can have dramatic results in these situations. Discipline the thought processes to think like the person you want to be and not the person you perceive yourself as being. Never use expressions such as "I can't do it." Instead replace them with expressions such as "I can't do it yet." And then focus your mind on positive images of yourself in the required situation. When you first read this paragraph many of you will shy from what it says as you mind feeds you negative thoughts about changing what are the weakest and most vulnerable areas of your lives. Be prepared for this and once again recognize that this is a negative response and it will need to be drowned by positive thoughts.

One of the most powerful tools for developing positive thinking is that of gratitude. Before we started trying to correct our thinking we tended to drift through life absorbing all the negative things that surround us and happened to us whilst disregarding the myriad of wonderful things that we are exposed every day. To actively search out things to be grateful for and focus on them, even if only briefly, can do wonders for our mental well being. We have been feeding our minds with positive thoughts about ourselves and our circumstances but that can become a little self-absorbing after a while. Instead try taking a slightly broader view and being grateful for things that previously were overlooked. Personally this has led me toward a much greater awareness of nature. Often when stuck in traffic I am able to see some flower or plant from the window of my stationary car and I focus briefly on that and the sheer wonder of it being there. Sunshine is another thing that I had simply been overlooking whilst blindfolded by negativity. From our health to our friends and family we all have things about us that we should be grateful for and training the mind to recognize opportunities for gratitude is possibly the most easy to use tool on the road to a more positive life. The mere fact that we are sleeping under a roof and not going to bed hungry at least three times per week puts us ahead of a huge percentage of the world's population. Learning to be grateful for things like that is a form of wealth in itself.

" In order to carry a positive action we must develop here a positive vision."

Dalai Lama.

## Chapter 11: Emotional Intelligence

The concept of emotional intelligence (EI) or emotional quotient (EQ) was created by the earlier work of two researchers, namely; Peter Salovey and John Mayer. However, it was not fully acknowledged until Daniel Goleman, an American psychologist, featured it in his book titled: "Emotional Intelligence - Why It Can Matter More Than IQ" 1995. Since then, the popularity of the concept has grown and is becoming more critical with the development of our nation. His spotlight was part of the reason emotional intelligence gained the attention of other psychologists, and people in general, which prompted subsequent studies and researches.

The question that readily comes to mind is: What is Emotional Intelligence? Emotional Intelligence is the ability to identify, recognize, understand, and manage one's emotions and others'. In other words, EI is simply the ability to:

•Identify, understand and manage our own emotions

•Recognize, understand and influence the emotions of others

The above sounds simple and basic. Yes actually, but it doesn't come easily, it is an art to be learned consciously. There are individual efforts to be made to have a full grasp of the concept.

To a more considerable extent, what happened to us in life is what we cannot control, although, there is always another option. But the good thing is that we can manipulate how, and to what extent these circumstances of life affect us. How well can you handle failure or disappointments depend mainly on the level of your emotional intelligence. Sometimes, victims of extreme emotional destabilization contemplate suicide. Such thoughts may keep pervading their mind. As the questions within them keep popping, their minds keep getting wrong answers when the need arises. This will adversely affect their judgment and little wonder why they put the unexpected into action eventually.

Emotional quotient varies in individuals. To some, the slightest wind of provocation will snatch their caution, while some will take a wilder and fiercer wind to be moved. However, being emotionally intelligent is not a gift, or a talent, neither an innate ability nor a quality that can be transmitted genetically. Rather, it is something to be mastered and well understood; after all, the environment we dwell in is our teacher!

Emotional intelligence is a choice. You can choose not to possess the skill. But it is safer to have it as it equips us with another arsenal to face the uncertainties life throws at us. Emotional intelligence is essential because as individuals, our success and the success of our career/work-life today depend on our ability to read other people's signals and react appropriately to them.

To this end, it is essential that each one of us must develop the mature emotional intelligence skills required to understand better, empathize and negotiate with other people — particularly as the economy has become more global. Otherwise, success will elude us in our lives and careers.

Elements of Emotional Intelligence

Daniel Goleman developed a framework of five core skills that defined emotional intelligence. These five skills can pair up into two primary competencies: personal competence (Dealing with yourself) and social or interpersonal competence. (Dealing with others)

Personal skills

•Self-awareness

•Self-regulation

•Motivation

Interpersonal skills

•Empathy

•Social skills

Self-awareness: This is the ability to identify your emotions and how they affect you. It requires paying optimal attention to your environment, your body, and mind. It is essential for personal development. It gives you a greater understanding of yourself and how you relate with others. When you are self-aware, you pay attention to your feelings, values, habits, personality, emotions, needs, strengths, and weaknesses. You have the good self-understanding and a deep sense of who you are. It will also help you to understand your emotions and how easily they get triggered. In the same token, to develop self-awareness requires tuning in to your true feelings. This is premised on the fact that if you evaluate your emotions, you can manage them. In addition to this, you will know your breaking point. In the real sense, the truth is that everyone has a breaking point, as there is a certain extent or a limit to which we can be emotionally stressed. If the limit is passed, one might be broken, and if overstretched, shattered.

If you flare up easily, you should have the idea of your own limit, and work towards taming the anger that pulls you out of your cool self. If someone or something is pushing you towards it, you would have understood that it is a cue to retreat or find another way(s) around it. This is Self-awareness. Self-awareness is a fundamental skill for personal development and good interpersonal relationship. When you are self-aware, you have a greater understanding of yourself and how you interact with others. It makes you pay attention to your feelings, values, lifestyle, character, emotions, desires, strengths, and weaknesses. You have the better self-understanding and a deep sense of who you are. You take note of your reactions to the things that have a direct effect on you and the people around you. The knowledge of self-awareness can lead us to more life satisfaction, better life choices, and overall success in both our private and professional field and even as a parent.

Self-regulation: This is connected to self-awareness as you need to be aware of the 'triggers' and your breaking points before you can know what, how, and when to regulate them. It simply means staying in control, mostly, helping yourself to decide against something that automatically happens when you get subjected to certain circumstances.

For example, if you are vulnerable at the sight of soda, even though your doctor advised you to abstain from taking it, due to particular health conditions. There is self-awareness already, backed with the doctor's suggestion/advise, but it will take optimal self-control or regulation to restrain yourself from yielding to the urge to take it when it is being served at a friend's party. Self-regulation would probably prompt you to go for water or anything but not soda.

Furthermore, while it is true that one often has little control over what he/she experiences emotionally; however, one can develop a management skill to regulate how long an emotion will last by using several techniques to reduce negative emotions such as anger, anxiety or depression. Some experts have identified techniques used among people at various times to deal with such conditions above, which include recasting a situation in a more positive light, taking a long walk and meditation or prayer. They have also submitted that self-regulation will involve the following properties:

Self-control: Managing disruptive impulses

Trustworthiness: Maintaining standards of honesty and integrity

Conscientiousness: Taking responsibility for your own performance

Adaptability: Handling change with flexibility

Innovation; Being open to new ideas

Motivation: Motivation is a driving tool in human endeavors. It keeps us plugged in. Never stay away from what keeps you connected; therefore, having proper knowledge of what drives you is very important towards achieving an emotionally stable and intelligent state.

It is, however, essential to note that motivating yourself for any achievement will require having some clear goals on your part and a positive attitude. While it may be that you have a predisposition to either a positive or a negative attitude. Naturally, as a person due to several factors, you can with effort and practice learn to think more positively by catching negative thoughts as they occur and reframing them in more concrete terms. This will help in so many ways of achieving your goals. Therefore motivation is made up of:

Achievement drive: Striving always to improve or to meet a standard of excellence.

Commitment: Aligning with the purposes of the group or organization.

Initiative: Readying yourself to act on opportunities.

Optimism: Pursuing goals persistently despite obstacles and setbacks.

Empathy: By default, humans are quick to criticize the slightest flop we can discover from something or someone. That single flop gets all the attention, and the other thousand jobs well done are swept under the carpet. Only if we could take time to process events that occur in our lives, then, less misunderstanding will occur. Empathy involves the ability to understand the feelings of others about a situation.

Empathy is putting on another person's shoe. If you can walk a fraction of kilometer in it, then, you will be slow to conclude and judge. Like someone once advised, "If you are offended and at the verge of losing your cool, make an excuse for the cause of it, and before you know it, your mind is wrapped around the reason, and the anger is dissolved. After all, there are three sides to a story: your side; their side; and the truth. If time is taken to put the sides together and get a three-dimensional view, it may dawn on you that your overreaction may not be necessary. A great deal of confusion can be eliminated by just taking the time to understand someone else's point of view before trying to convince them of your idea.

How to Improve Your Empathy

You cannot give what you don't have; there is no way compassion can spring out of emptiness. Empathy starts with you; you need to begin the practice of empathy with yourself, by pursuing your emotional desires, knowing when it is realistic and when it is not, and going against the wind when necessary, as long as you can handle the situation.

Pay attention to body language: Your body tells more on how you feel about a situation than your voice. When someone crosses his arms, moves his feet back and forth, or bite his lips in silence, it means something. This gesture means certain things are going in the mind. Be on the lookout for those signs if you want to understand people better. This can help in responding accordingly to a situation.

Respond to the feelings of others: Since emotional quotient is about how you feel and how others (around you) feel, try to understand what they are going through before you act.

Social skills: Whatever the situation is, one need to learn how to do a seeming difficult thing- Be as open to hearing positive feedbacks as to negative ones. Life is Uncertain. Besides, how you relate to others is essential.

Honing Your Social Skills

To develop social skills, you have to practice the habit consistently. Initially, it may not be easy, but with regular practice, it becomes second nature which comes effortlessly. In emotional intelligence, the essence of social skill is to be able to bring people together, sacrificing your comfort for the benefits of others. Focusing on what the team wants. You are mainly driven by the shine and success of others instead of yours because once you push someone further, there is no way that person would be better than you. Developing social skills is about being aware of how we communicate with others.

## Chapter 12: Master Social Skills

Any time you are in an environment where you have to interact with other people there is nothing more important than having good social skills. After all, if you can't communicate clearly with others, or you remain detached and aloof from those around you, your chances of success will suffer dramatically. This is especially true in any job that requires a team-oriented approach to accomplish tasks. The more you have to rely on the assistance or efforts of others, the more you need to be able to interact with them in a real and meaningful way. If you can't communicate your ideas clearly and effectively you won't be able to turn those ideas into reality.

Alternatively, if you can't understand what others are trying to convey you won't be able to produce the results they are looking for. This means that communication needs to be a two-way street. Not only do you need to make your ideas understood, but you also need to be able to understand the ideas and goals of others. Only when everyone involved can understand each other and the tasks at hand can a team have any chance of being successful. Therefore, if you want to increase your emotional intelligence it is critical that you master social skills.

Improve communication with others

Mastering social skills begins with the basic element of communication. No amount of positive interaction with people will be significant if it causes confusion or uncertainty. Again, one of the most important aspects of emotional intelligence is to reduce those factors that create negative emotions in the first place. Things like confusion, misunderstanding and doubt only serve to create the stress and anxiety that makes emotional intelligence harder to master. Therefore, it is vital that you improve your communication with others.

The first step in this process is to take the time to speak in a clear manner. All too often people rush through communications in an attempt to save time. Unfortunately, this usually leads to mistakes being made as a result of people being unsure of what they are supposed to do. Thus, rather than saving time, rushed communications, whether spoken or written, can actually cause problems and delays that take more time to fix. However, if you take the time to get your ideas across clearly you can save time by avoiding misunderstandings and the mistakes they can create.

Even if you speak in a clear and concise manner, others may not actually follow what you are trying to say. Therefore, it is also vital that you take the time to ask people you speak to whether or not they fully understand what you are saying. Getting their feedback in the moment will go a long way towards eliminating the confusion and uncertainty that can cause unnecessary stress and anxiety. Furthermore, by soliciting feedback you will increase the other person's sense of self-worth. The more you value their opinion, the more they will feel valued overall.

Another critical element for improved communication is the balance between passion and knowledge. Every time you talk to someone make sure you show positive emotional energy regarding the matter at hand. You won't get the other person interested in what you are saying if you aren't interested in it yourself. Additionally, make sure you are well informed regarding the matter at hand. If you seem unsure about your position, or how to accomplish the task at hand, you will only create doubt and frustration in the minds of others. Thus, good communication isn't just about speaking clearly, it's also about speaking passionately and with conviction.

Develop a strong sense of empathy

The most effective people in terms of social skills are those who possess a strong sense of empathy. This is also true as regards to emotional intelligence. One of the most effective ways of being emotionally intelligent is to understand your emotional perspective as well as the emotional perspective of those around you. In a way, this is the ability to enter another person's mind and see things through their eyes. The more you practice empathy, the more effective you will become at any type of interaction with other people.

This skill is critical whether you are a boss or a regular employee. Sometimes a boss might come across as overly critical of your performance, raising their voice, appearing agitated and showing general frustration with you. If you take their behavior at face value you will only become anxious and defensive as a result. However, if you take a moment to consider things from their perspective you will realize just how desperate they actually are. More often than not your bosses have to answer bosses of their own, meaning that they have to answer for each and every setback encountered along the way. Subsequently, they are wholly dependent on your performance in order to achieve their goals. If your efforts aren't quite right, they will have to pay the price.

Once you realize that their aggression is actually a sign of desperation you can better understand their behavior. Subsequently, rather than becoming defensive or hurt you can seek to assure them that any mistakes will be corrected in a timely manner. Additionally, you can reassure them that you are wholly committed to the task in hand and that you desire success as much as they do. By responding this way, you will demonstrate that you are on their side, and that you are a part of the solution rather than a part of the problem. This will go a long way to calming their mood, which will improve your interaction with them exponentially.

## Chapter 13: Working on emotional intelligence

Emotional intelligence is thought to exist in four key elements - self-awareness, self-management, empathy and social awareness and interpersonal relationship skills.

Let's take a look at each element for some ideas on how to work on these.

**Self-Awareness** is our ability to read and understand our own emotions and the impact these can have on our relationships and self-worth.

Do you know what makes you tick? What are your goals and ambitions?

Ask people for feedback on your strengths and weaknesses, how they would describe you and what they think your goals/interests are. If this sounds too scary then try some online personality tests and collect a list of recurring attributes.

Take a few minutes each day to write down some reflections at the beginning or end of the day. If you find writing tough, record a minute-long video on your phone and listen back the day afterward.

Spending a little time thinking about what is really important to you and writing down a plan or goals really helps to build up that core sense of self. Believe it or not, we are all working towards something - learning a new skill, saving to buy something, working on your physique, improving relationships with family, working towards a healthy retirement, reading more, it could be anything.

Once we have an idea of who we are we can start to look at how we can manage ourselves and our interactions with others.

Self-management techniques are your own set of tools to help you develop a goal plan and control disruptive emotions and impulses that could set you off course.

Having a clear plan provides a point of focus, allowing you to prioritise tasks and ensure that none of the self-care basics such as exercise or relaxation time fall off the radar. Start small on the more difficult tasks and work on them regularly until they become habit.

Emotionally, self-management is about working on your mindset, managing emotions and increasing confidence. Spending a little time on yourself by creating a morning routine is one way to increase positivity and help you cross off some self-care straight away. Exercising, journaling, meditation and repeating morning affirmations are all good choices.

Mindfulness is a great way to give yourself some distance to work through emotions and can take as much or little time as you need.

The five senses mindfulness technique is a stressbuster. Use it when patience is in short supply or for a quick breather on hectic days.

The Five Senses Technique

Find an inside or outside space where you can sit comfortably for a few minutes. You are aiming to spend approx. 30 seconds with each sense.

Close your eyes and start to focus on your breath. Take a few slow breaths and once you feel ready begin to listen and take notice of what you can hear. Try to listen past the closest sounds to what you can hear beyond.

Next turn your attention to what you can smell. It might not be a recognisable scent, it could be fresh, smoky, the smell of food or perfume.

Again spend approx. 30 seconds here and then begin to move your tongue slightly as you think about what you can taste. It could be the remnants of your last drink or food that you've eaten. It could be the sensation of sweetness or bitterness.

Now we'll move to touch. Without moving them, notice the weight of your hands resting on your knees or lap. Feel the material of your clothes over your skin and the support of the seat or floor beneath you. If you are outdoors, you may feel the air moving around you with a breeze or the warmth of sunshine.

Finally open your eyes and look around you. Find an object to focus on and take in everything about its appearance. Is it moving or still? It's depth of colour, size, shape. Is it opaque or transparent? What is it made of? Is it patterned or plain?

Return your focus to your breath and have a gentle stretch.

How do you feel?

The purpose of this practice is to allow your body and mind time to settle into calm, while you are busy focusing on each of the senses. It is a great way to approach self-management, with the idea behind this being to prevent you from getting to a stage of overwhelm. Keep on top of it and be rewarded with a clearer mind, better stress coping abilities and productive power.

**Empathy & Social awareness** is the ability to understand the needs of those around you, along with an awareness of how others are feeling (empathy).

Digital communication and social media have some explaining to do, with research showing that we are less empathic today than just a few decades ago. A simple side effect of this is that we are less trusting, not great for business or personal relationships. When we can demonstrate our understanding of someone's needs and show consideration for their feelings, we gain their trust. By building trust, we build credibility and positive connections.

Listen attentively to others, time is our most valuable resource and most people do appreciate being given another's full attention if only for a few minutes, so put the phone away.

Learn from others by watching their interactions and squirrelling the notes away in your brain for a future situation. What do they do differently? Did their response work well?

We all have varying emotional states and coping abilities. If you aren't sure how to approach someone, make a mental note of how they are responding to others and the language they are using. Then adapt your approach and sensitivity accordingly.

**Interpersonal relationship skills** are what we use to communicate with others.

None of us are born with these skills, they are learned and improved through practice and through making mistakes.

Good communication is key to any relationship and like empathy, our communication skills are being re-tuned through the increasing use of modern technology.

The development of interpersonal skills is however just as important to ensure your messages are conveyed effectively and without causing conflict. This is where our self-management techniques can help us, by ensuring we take that step back while figuring out how to manage our emotions effectively.

→Consider your non-verbal communication - appearance, dress, body language and facial expressions all contribute to the non-verbal message that we are sending out. Work out how you want to be seen and take steps towards this presentation.

→ Be accountable and take responsibility for your actions. If you make a mistake, owning up to it and apologising actually increases your credibility.

→ Maintaining a positive outlook helps you appear approachable to others. Focusing on the positive will help you as much as others. Exchanging pleasantries at work is a really easy way to keep communication open between colleagues. Saying your p's and q's are another painless sign of respect that people really do appreciate. Reserve complaining for occasional use. Would you rather chew something over with a cheerful person or a grumpy person?

→ Paying attention to others shows them that you care. Really listen to what they have to say and provide support where you can.

→Keep your sparkle - Your personality is unique and valuable. Although society does dictate certain behaviours such as polite language and general consideration. That said it can be taken too far which could end up with a race of robot-style humans.

## Chapter 14: Social Management and Responsibility

The terms Social management and responsibility refer to a group or organization's participation in environmental, ethical, and social issues outside of the organization itself. 'Outside of the organization' can refer to issues at the country level, B2B (Business to Business) level or even the individual development of the members within the group or organization.

Benefits of Emotional Intelligence

Emotional intelligence is "the ability to perceive emotions, to access and generate emotions so as to assist thought, to understand emotions and emotional knowledge, and to reflectively regulate emotions so as to promote emotional and intellectual growth (Mayer-Salovey, Four Branch Model of Emotional Intelligence).

Focusing on the importance of Emotional Intelligence and developing 'EI' skills serves many benefits. Specifically, it affects one decision-making ability, relationships, and health.

**Decision-making.** Having an awareness of your emotions, where they come from and what they mean, can allow you to take a more rational, well-planned approach to how you are going to make a specific decision.

**Relationships.** When one is able to understand why they are the way they are and why they react to things the way they do, they tend to gain more of an appreciation for others and who they are, which can in turn lead to stronger relationships, business and personal.

**Health.** Many times, internal turmoil expresses itself as physical illnesses. Always harboring negative emotions can lead to higher stress levels in the body, which can temporarily or fatally damage it.

## Articulate your Emotions Using Language

As a child, it may be acceptable to 'act out your emotions' to get your point across, but when you become an adult it is frowned upon and certainly not appropriate in the work place. Emotions will never go away, but that is not an excuse to say, do and behave anyway we want to. It is important to understand your emotions, what they are, and why you feel that way, and then share your feelings via positive and constructive conversation.

When in a leadership role, you may encounter several opportunities to express yourself, whether it is praising a worker for a job well done, or reprimanding an employee for not meeting deadline. But the key to making sure you articulate your emotions in an effective and efficient manner is to channel those emotions so that your message comes across as firm but professional.

Practical Illustration

Katie knew that the emotional intelligence levels within her office were lacking. To increase these, she had a meeting to explain the importance of them. She taught that emotional intelligence has an effect on the company as a whole, as well as the individual members that make it run. If each person is well practiced in decision making, good habits within their relationships, and an overall control of their stressors and anger, they are more emotionally intelligent. After working on these aspects, the office was better able to deal with internal and external conflict and development, leading to a stronger company.

## Chapter 15: Is it Really Possible to Improve Your Emotional Intelligence?

Can your EQ really be improved? In dealing with other people whether in school, office or even in relationships, it is very important to be armed with a good level of emotional intelligence. You can attend some coaching seminars on how to improve your EQ but then, is there a hundred percent assurance it will really improve? It's been said that while IQ cannot be improved, EQ can. Just practice regularly until you attain the level of intelligence that will be beneficial in your everyday interactions.

Here are some points of consideration in improving your EQ;

The level of your EQ is compact, but not stiff.

The ability to recognize and handle your emotions is reasonably steady over a period of time. It is prejudiced by your genetics and upbringing experiences. But that doesn't necessarily mean you cannot in any way change it. In reality, improvements are achievable with an infinite deal of endurance and supervision. People can change but the question is the willingness to try.

Excellent training programs will work for you.

Since it is not impossible to improve your EQ, several training programs have been conducting seminar and coaching on ways to improvement. You would just have to be wise in choosing which one will work well for you. A very important factor to consider in choosing a program is your belief in the speaker or coach. You have to trust completely that he will do miracles for you EQ.

Improvement through precise feedback

Most of the time, you are not aware how others regard you. You may not feel that you are actually nice and think that other people think so too, thus resulting to a low EQ. There are some though that regards themselves as very confident and great so they live up to that belief not knowing it is the opposite.

Several coaches and techniques are better than others.

It is always advisable to check on the training programs first before joining one. That way, you will be more able to choose effectively which will suit you best.

A number of people are easier to coach than others.

There are times when even the most patient or the best coach / speaker will not be successful in improving one's EQ. This is because every individual has a different level of catching up. Some may get it real fast but some may take much time towards improvement.

## Chapter 16: Emotions and How to Command and Master Them

Do you let emotions take you over? Do you allow your emotions to destroy your life slowly? If so then listen up. The first step in learning to command and master your emotions is to understand the source. Emotions stem from feelings, heart, and psyche. Therefore, we must understand emotions, heart, feelings, and psyche to come to a point of acceptance.

Emotions: Emotions are at times complexity, since the responses come from a set state of mind. Physiological changes sometimes take place as the emotions response. The emotions work jointly with the minds conscious. This response promotes our sensitive feelings. Some of those feelings sparked from emotions include, anger, fear, joy, sadness, happiness. The underlying sources, such as beliefs, teachings, learning, etc all contribute to how the emotions response. The emotions create changes, which presents self in emotional, emotionalism, emotionalist, emotionalize, emotionless, and emotive.

The state of mind where a person is emotional displays sensitive to a response. In other words, the person likely does not like what he is seeing or hearing and responds on the emotions rather than thoughts. At the point, the person is displaying higher value placed on the emotions, which leads to an emotionalism state of mind. If the person response with anger, thus this person illustrates emotional-emotionalism-emotionalist response, since his emotions are excessively acting out and seen in the behavior, conduct, thoughts, or language. Now, if the person acts out thoughtfully, he is demonstrating an emotionalized state of mind.

Thus, he separates feelings, emotions, and thoughts. Emotive people tend to relate to the emotions, yet they express emotions from triggers or arousers. Feelings: Feelings are physical basic sense. In other words, the body response to touches while recognizing sensations. This is an aware and recognized response. Now on the emotional level, feelings are states of reactions. For instance, she showed joy from his remark. This is a response known as compassion, sparked from sensational feelings. Now if a person is susceptible to the impressions of others, thus sensitivity sparks the emotions, which gives rise to feelings. For instance, she felt overwhelmed and deeply hurt at his statement. This is an overly sensitive emotion. The emotions are conflicting or opposite backdrops of the mind (psyche). That is the emotions contrast from the awareness of the mind. This means that the emotions separate from the mind's thoughts, perceptions, and recognized sensations. On the other hand, the mind can work with the mind by illustrating high awareness through acknowledgement. Examples of emotional response both commanded and non-commanded:

A woman response emotional to the touch of the man, yet although she is married she, response to the touch and gives into his desires: We know where this is going. The woman is allowing her emotions to control her, rather than thinking of the consequences of her adulterous behaviors. The man is also giving into his emotions, therefore no commanding or mastering of the emotions exists in this situation. The woman touched him desirously; he pulls away from her touch and explains to the woman assertively and responsibly that he is already taken.

She tries to persuade him; yet again, he pulls away and stresses his place, while slowly moving away from the woman. This man is showing control of his emotions and desires. Thus, he has command and masters his mind. In both illustrations, you see, desire, feelings, emotions, thoughts, sensations, and so forth. This brings us to the psyche. The psyche is the conscious mind, which presents awareness. While I will not break off into defining the awareness and conscious mind, I will say that by now you should see what is needed to command and master your emotions.

Now we can see that the heart is where the personality stems, as well as where considerations, compassion, love, emphatic, sympathy, affection, and the like all come from. Pull this heart together with emotions, mind, and feelings and what do you come up with; can you see it? Physiological changing is part of understanding how to command and master your emotions.

## Chapter 17: Essential Keys for Commanding Your Emotions

When you can learn to master your emotions, you can ultimately master your life. It is vital that you understand the reasons why you do the things that you do because of an inner drive to change the way you feel. For example, if you want to make more money, lose weight, or buy new clothes, you are doing this because of the feeling you get when you accomplish your goals. People who believe that losing weight will help them to become more confident, and ultimately attract love into their life, will go the extra mile to shed off unwanted pounds.

Emotions are an essential part of our life. Rather than putting them off and hiding them, you need to acknowledge them and realize the truth that lies within them.

The Emotional Triad

No matter the situation that you might find yourself in, there are three main factors that will determine your feelings about the situation. Psychologists refer to these factors as the Emotional Triad, and they include the following:

Your Physiology

Every single emotion that you experience in your life is first felt in your body. For example, if you want to feel more confident, then you need to be grounded, principled, and courageous in your speech. On the other hand, if you're going to feel more passion in your life, then you should start talking and moving more rapidly. For those people who want to feel depressed, simply have to frown, breathe shallowly, slump over, and stare at the ground. The bottom line is that the manner in which you use your body will end up changing how you feel. Emotion is created by motion.

What You Focus On

Along with how you use your body, what you focus on will also determine how you feel. If you want to feel happy, you need to focus your attention on things that make you happy. By recalling more joyful moments in your past, you can create a platform and an opportunity to be happy today. When you remove all the good things and experiences in your life and focus on the negative, you will most certainly end up feeling depressed. In life, both good things and bad things are available, and it is up to you to decide what you want to focus on.

Your Language

The words that you use have the ability to change the way you feel. If you begin making statements like, "I'm exhausted," or "I'm so bored," the chances are that you will feel tired or bored. Every single word that you speak has an emotional state attached to it. Some words that you use are disempowering, while others are encouraging and uplifting. By exercising care over your vocabulary, statements, metaphors, and phrases, you can control and command your emotions.

The reality of the Emotional Triad is that happiness is a choice, and the same goes for anger, depression, and frustration. There isn't anyone who can make you feel angry or happy, but rather, it depends on how you interpret every situation that you face in your life.

How to Deal with Negative Emotions

Both negative and positive emotions are a part of our lives and can't simply be wished away. However, you can decide to deal with these emotions so that you can effectively suppress the negative ones and encourage positive emotions. There are four ways in which you can deal with your negative emotions.

Avoidance

Avoidance simply means keeping away from situations that have the potential to trigger negative emotions. For example, you might avoid approaching strangers or taking risks because you fear rejection or failure. It is incredibly common for people to turn to self-medication, like alcohol food, or drugs, to ward off negative emotions, which is just another form of avoidance.

Denial

Denial is the process of disassociating yourself from the negative emotions you're feeling by using statements like, "It wasn't that bad." While you may think that it is perfectly alright for you to go into denial about your negative emotions, the approach, unfortunately, will increase those negative emotions and will continue to intensify them until you pay attention to the negative emotions.

Learning and Using Your Negative Emotions

Learning from your negative emotions and using them to your advantage is one of the methods used to deal with negative emotions. First, you need to come to the understanding that all your emotions, both negative and positive, are there to serve you. Your daily emotions are a guideline, a support system, or a call to action. They tell you that the activity that you are participating in either works or it doesn't.

The thing that you need to remember is that you are the origin of all of your emotions and that you and you alone create them. You don't need a particular reason to feel a certain way, but rather it is all your choice. The power to command your emotions lies within you. Every emotion comes from you, and you are the only one who is suited to not only handle them but subdue them as well. With continued practice, you can take advantage of your emotions and have them work for you rather than against you.

## Chapter 18: What's Your Point of View

We must accept life for what it is — a challenge. You actually end up achieving your dreams by conquering your greatest fears. Remember, one step, one moment, then the next step and its moment. To live a psychologically meaningful life, there must be in one's heart a genuine love of truth, for the meaning we attribute to life will determine our behavior.

Improving oneself requires a great deal of concentration. The task is hard work, but with concentration comes greater insight, faster development, and stronger motivation. How we behave in the world is largely determined by our beliefs that have become general truths. We navigate life with our beliefs. The problem is that some of our beliefs can be rigid, inaccurate or inappropriate, and may hurt us rather than help us. At different times in our lives, we need to reevaluate our values and beliefs and determine their positive and negative points. Your point of view on life determines the quality of your life.

Wake up with an attitude of gratitude.

Mental Fitness

Everything in life has purpose, but knowledge of that purpose makes us able to use it to our best advantage. We carve out our own destiny — we make ourselves what we are. Each person has roughly 28,000 days to live. So, how do you want to live your life? We each have a life to live, one that has purpose and meaning. Life consists of what a person is thinking of all day. Maintaining mental fitness is a process and hard work.

When you accept yourself just as you are, then you can change. Life is one huge on-going negotiation. You are responsible for your happiness, pleasure and mental health.

You end up achieving your dreams by going through the doors of your greatest fears. One step, one moment, then the next step and its moment. To live a psychologically meaningful life, there must be in one's heart a genuine love of truth; the meaning we attribute to life determines our behavior.

**Recipe**

Step on the stone as it appears.

Take responsibility for what you want and need.

Avoid negative people.

Look at problems as challenges

Identify your strengths

Control yourself. Look for solutions. Delete problems.

Understand the connectedness between how you think, feel and behave.

Seek balance in all you do.

"If I chose to concentrate on extending compassion instead of judgment, how would my experience change?"

Base Line Reality

One third of the population likes you. One third of the population dislikes you. One third of the population is indifferent to you or just doesn't care. Your job is to stick with the people who like you and forget the rest. Not everyone will like you or love you - It doesn't matter how cute you are. A big so what!

According to Drs. Everly and Mitchell, over seven billion people are in the world - 3% of the7 billion people are psychotic. 7% of the people are neurotic. 75-85% are normal. 7% are above average and 3% are superior psychologically. This is about mental health, not money. Every moment of life is an opportunity and the greatest opportunity is to know the value of opportunity.

Recipe

Be open.

Be creative.

Be sensitive to others.

Be patient.

Be careful.

Be fair.

Don't harm anyone.

Be honest. Be aware of your intentions

Be yourself.

Don't jump through your butt to please people – please yourself.

Find the balance between trust and suspicion.

Go Inward.

Living Life

Has your relationship recently ended? Don't like your job? Need a job? It's stressful. Not all stress is bad. It's a signal that something needs to be done. Stress is the way we respond to change. Most people think of stress as negative. But your body cannot tell the difference between a positive or negative stressor. Emotional signs of stress are bad temper, depression, mood swings, irritability, anxiety, being easily discouraged, feeling demoralized; this is normal stress. Critical stress is apathy, loss of emotional control, panic states, depression, rage and suicidal thoughts. Don't ignore the warning signs within yourself. Listen to your body. You are as you think. Put stress to work for you. When under stress, clean up the mess. Do something!

Our stress triangle, the head, neck and shoulders are where we hold a lot of our tension. But our muscles tighten to protect us. These tightened muscles hold that position — the fight-or-flight syndrome. When this happens, get a massage or just do some stretching exercises. People who do something positive about problems are most likely to successfully respond to psychological stress. Joy is often the ability to be happy in small ways.

Life is like a blind date; sometimes you have to have a little faith. There is only one of you; now and forever, you are in control of your personal experience. When you wake up in the morning and gingerly pop out of bed, wake up with an attitude of gratitude. You are born again! Then ask yourself, "What am I willing to do today?" "What do I want to see happen?"

You are in control of your happiness. You have the power to change anything about yourself. Don't sit around mumbling, "Poor Me, Poor Me, Pour me a Drink." Self-pity is a waste of time. The more fully we give our energy, the more it returns to us. In your personal drama, you are sharing the stage with everyone else you meet today.

**Recipe**

Trust your hopes, not your fears.

Learn to respond, not react.

What we do today is what matters most

Exercise, rest, and eat healthful foods.

Choose your attitude and direction.

Pain is inevitable – misery is optional.

Be nice to yourself.

Avoid the "Try Hards" or over pushing, and over trying.

Don't let situations dictate your behavior.

Wait-Think-Respond. Waiting helps thinking. Thinking increases the correct response. Pause.

Develop your sense of humor.

 "Peace comes from within me, and is not determined by people, places, or things."

Internal Balancing

Stress is like snow it builds up. Don't choke back your feelings. Most people who choke back their feelings wind up having a heart attack in their 50s. Talk with a friend. Keep a journal. Go for a walk. Try crying. But don't cry on the train or the bus. Crying releases a lot of tension. Go see a light-hearted movie. Don't over protect yourself. What for? What's the payoff for being heavily defended and defensive? Evaluate yourself and ask for feedback. Find the balance between defensiveness and openness, and between trust and suspicion.

Our fate in life is a process that continues to emerge. When you accept yourself just as you are, then you can change. Life is one huge on-going negotiation. Pay attention to what you want and need. Embrace all of today. It takes strength to manage difficulties. Lack of strength equals failure. We need to develop coping and resiliency skills to deal with your internal and external life. You can change your mind. You don't have to live or die with every decision. Be flexible.

**Recipe**

You can decide even if you don't have the perfect answer.

What is the worst that can happen?

What are your options?

Walk straight "fear-ward".

Listen to yourself.

What are your self-defeating thoughts?

You can heal what you feel.

Question Your Thinking

Don't give yourself bad information. Life consists of what a person is thinking of all day. What you are thinking about every second of your life is your true reality. A person needs to understand the connectedness between how he or she thinks, feels, and behaves. How you think affects your feelings. Your feelings affect your behavior. Question yourself. Challenge yourself. This may be difficult since you may be asking yourself for insight that you might not have. Ask for feedback from others on your current thought.

Think in opposites...180 degrees. This is oppositional thinking. Practice this concept. Practice positive self-talk. If you say something negative about yourself, say two positive things about yourself. Negate your negative thinking with positive thinking.

**Recipe**

Your foreground is connected to your background.

What thought(s) are you living with from an earlier time?

When your feel unsure about something - examine the consequences.

What am I telling myself?

What are you thinking about all day? Happy thoughts? Angry thoughts? Fearful thoughts?  Negative thoughts?

Thought draws the lines of fate.

Stay positive.

Small changes lead to larger changes.

One step, then the next step.

## Chapter 19: Sensing Your Employee's Emotions

So we have talked about the importance of managing yourself and your emotions, now we are going to talk about sensing and picking up on emotional signals that your employees will be giving you. Understanding these signals is a large part of emotional intelligence and will allow you to bond and understand your employees on a deeper level. The ability to create this bond will allow you to communicate and motivate your employees which will allow you to manage at a higher level. Being able to understand your employee's wants and needs will allow you to create a reward system that is tailored directly to them. This will increase productivity and improve the rate at which you hit goals and deadlines. A strong understanding of your employees, will allow them a higher level of comfort and they will be more open to discuss problems and solutions. This allows you fix any problems immediately and saves you work and headaches on the back end. Connecting and understanding your employees makes up a huge part of emotional intelligence so make sure you pay close attention.

Sensing Concerns And Problems With Your Employees

If you find that a certain employee is missing deadlines or targets, as a leader you need to take an active role in fixing this problem immediately. You need to have a one on one meeting with the employee and figure out the reason for the poor performance. There are two mistakes that poor managers will make when dealing with an employee who is missing targets. The first, they will wait and put off confronting the employee until the problem has grown out of control. As a leader, you need to learn how to face stress and difficult situations head on. Many problems can be solved if you act immediately. The second mistake that poor managers make is calling out poor performance in a group setting or meeting. Personal reasons could be the issue and embarrassing someone in front of others is a terrible thing to do. Make sure that every meeting that requires you to discuss poor performance is done in a one on one closed door environment. You need to be able to empathize with your employees and discuss any problem that both personal and work related. Understand where they are coming from and the steps that you can take to address the issue. Really dig down deep and try to find the root or source of the problem. This will allow you to really identify and connect with your employee on a deep level. Some problems are avoided because employees feel they have nobody to talk to. This is an office environment that you need to avoid. If you are going to become a leader with emotional intelligence you need to be able to sense problems, communicate on a deeper level, and take steps to address the problem.

Being Able To Recognize Customer and Client                                    Needs
 This trait is tied into sensing and taking advantage of opportunities. To run a successful company you need to be able to anticipate and fulfill your clients or customer's needs. Putting yourself in your client's shoes and recognizing their needs and desires will allow you to sense opportunities and capture them when the time comes. Understanding your client base will allow you to properly strategize and create a game plan to satisfy their need or problem. All great businesses solve a problem and you need to be able to sense new problems and create new plans. So how do you sense client's needs before they make them explicit? Well, this

skill is what separates mediocre managers and leaders from great ones. You once again need to communicate on an emotional level to really understand and satisfy their needs. The best way to get this accomplished is to ask open ended questions. Asking open ended questions is a popular sales technique, used to get the customer talking, which allows them to divulge their problems. This allows the salesmen to interpret those problems and tailor their sales pitch, making it seem like their product can solve the clients issues. If you are going to be able to spot client problems you need to utilize the same technique.

Open ended questions are designed to get a client talking. The more the client talks the better the chances you have of uncovering needs and wants. Essentially, an open ended question is a question that cannot be answered in a simple yes or no. The client will have to elaborate and craft a long drawn out answer. Open ended questions will generally start with How, What, Why, and When. For example, What are your thoughts on our new product? Why did you not buy our other product? When was the last time you saw a product like this one? How is your business doing in this economy? All these questions cannot be answered with a simple yes or no. They are designed to get the client talking and stating problems that you can solve. Once the client starts talking, you job is to shut up and listen, don't make the mistake of interrupting your client when he is giving you valuable information. This is just one technique you can use to uncover needs and build rapport with client. By understanding your client's needs, you are in a position to spot opportunities and better serve your entire client base.

Developing and Mentoring Your Employees

We mentioned in the beginning of this book the successful emotional intelligence model that companies are looking to implement. This model begins with hiring employees who show basic signs of emotional intelligence and are willing to work at improving their skills. These employees are then presented with an entry level job in which they can work and cultivate their emotional intelligence. Then when the time comes, they are promoted to a management position where they are allowed to test out their emotional intelligence skills. This process is all well and good, but it has one step that absolutely needs to be followed, these employees need someone to help them develop. This is where you come into the equation. You need to make it a priority to sit down, communicate, and improve the skills of your employees. You need to be proactive and make sure they are improving not only work related skills but emotional intelligence skills as well. A well trained workforce will allow them to use time more efficiently and improve their problem solving skills. But the key to this step is you need to be proactive. Employees are not going to go out of their way to improve or learn a new skill. As a manager you need to make this your priority that your office is always improving, and you are taking the proper amount of time to improve your employees.

One way to make sure that all your employees are receiving the time they need to learn and cultivate their skills, is to implement a mentorship program in your office. This will allow your new employees to receive hands on training from experienced employees, which allows both the new and experienced employees to benefit. The new employees are matched with a mentor which will allow them access to one on one coaching and mentoring. You would never have the time to be able to provide one on one mentoring to each of your employees unless you are in a really small business.

The experienced employees will be allowed to test out their management skills and learn how to handle employees on a small scale. Make sure both parties understand the work that is required and the benefits that they both will receive. Once again, communication is key during a mentorship program. You want to make sure your pair is a good fit and that work production is improving not decreasing. Make it a habit to meet with each mentorship pair at the end of the week to see exactly how things are progressing. The Ability To Inspire And Motivate The next trait that separates average managers from great ones, is the ability to motivate and inspire employees. You can come up with the best game plans and strategies, but if you fail to motivate and inspire your employees your work production and quality is going to be sub par. All great leaders throughout history had the ability to motivate and inspire their followers. If you are going to be great, you need to practice and hone this skill. Being able to motivate an audience or group of employees is not a skill that just appears overnight. Great football coaches spend years practicing motivational speeches and tactics. So if you are going to become an expert motivator, you are going to have to put in some work.

Motivating and inspiring your employees all comes down to one important concept. Can you create a team atmosphere so your employees feel that your goals are aligned? If you can align your employee's goals with your own, you will find that motivating and inspiring your employees will be much easier. Creating a unified vision is the number one way to motivate and inspire. Players will run any play a coach asks for no matter what, as long as they believe that the coach is aligned to win just like they want to. So once again, it all comes down to understanding your employees and their goals. If you can drill down and really figure out what motivates them, you can implement a powerful reward and incentive program. The problem with most reward and incentive programs that managers implement to improve production, is they implement rewards and bonuses that are not aligned to certain people's true desires. Some employees may want vacation days, others may want bonuses. It's your job as a leader and a manager to understand these needs and make sure you are aligned. This will allow you to inspire and motivate even the most difficult employees, and you will see office morale rise and productivity increase. Handling Change and The Ability To Keep Your Team Flexible One great quality of a leader with a strong emotional intelligence skill set, is the ability to remain flexible and keep your ego on the sideline. While this may be easy for you to, your team of employees may not be able to stay as flexible and

welcome change. Handling change can be difficult for any company, especially if the change you are going to be making goes against a long held company strategy or tradition. Some changes may not be met with enthusiasm and may foster resentment among employees. Changes with personnel, such as mass hiring and firings designed to shake up the company structure, can create a hostile work environment. Your job is keep emotions under control and make sure your employees embrace change and not oppose it.
 Whatever the change is going to be, make sure you have a reason why you think the change is necessary. If you can communicate the benefits of the change and why you are making it to your employees, you stand a better chance of uniting them and aligning them to your goals. The next step you want to complete is to make sure that you have a solid plan. Having a plan that will break down the

change into small increments and show the benefits of your new strategy, will be easier for your employees to digest. Make sure the plan is well thought out and detailed as well. If you can show your employees that you put thought and effort into your plan, you will have a better chance of aligning them as well. The worst thing you could do when implementing a change is to make the change without having a plan. This will make your decision look emotional and sloppy. Another common mistake to avoid, is when announcing the change make sure everyone is present. If some employees are left out of a the meeting, rumors can spread and you will lose the opportunity to make sure all your points come across clear and concise.

Being Able To Persuade Your Audience During some point in your managing career you are going to come across employees who do not share the same vision as you do. You are going to come to find that no matter how deep you connect with this individual, you are going to have differing views. In their opinion your game plan or strategy is wrong. They are willing to follow your strategy for fear of being fired, but you know that they are not going to put forth a solid effort and they risk hurting and lowering office morale. This is when you need to use the next emotional intelligence skill, persuasion. The ability to persuade is a common trait of all leaders. Whether they need to convince their troops to head into war, convince voters to vote for them, or convince employees that cutting bonuses will help the overall health of a company, having the ability to influence is one of the most powerful tools in a leader's arsenal.

We have talked about convincing your employees to join your side when discussing numerous different scenarios that you are going to encounter. The same concept applies to persuasion. You need to align yourself with your employee's views and then tailor your plan to benefit them. You want to link the features of your plan to the prospective benefits that your employee's will receive. For example, a presidential candidate is looking to secure votes from the middle class. He will announce his economic plan and the numerous tax relief features. For next few months all you will hear is how the new tax plan will benefit the middle class. How the tax break (features) can save middle class families $5,000 a year (benefits). The more specific and descriptive your link from features to benefits the better. If you can incorporate a story or two to really drive home your point and make an emotional connection, that's even better.

# Chapter 20: Education and Emotional Intelligence

How can we expect our youth to be good leaders if many of our educators and parents are not? Emotional intelligence helps us to form a strong foundation for making good life decisions. Studies show that at best, IQ only contributes about 20 percent to the factors that determine life success, leaving 80 percent to other forces.

We expect our youth to graduate from school with the tools necessary to be successful throughout life. Most of us can agree that these expectations are not being met. For example, South Carolina has a dropout rate somewhere between 35 % and 55 %. At a 50% dropout rate, the South Carolina economy is losing $273 million per year in revenue from lost wages, taxes and productivity for only one year of South Carolina high school dropouts. Multiply that by a 30-year lifetime and the costs to the South Carolina economy is $8.19 Billion for one lost class. We can multiply that cost by years of dropouts and then multiply it across the country.

Statistics also show that high school dropouts are 3.5 times more likely than high school graduates to be arrested and 8 times as likely to be in jail or prison. So when we add in the cost of jails, prisons, alcohol and drug abuse centers and mental institutions, we begin to get an understanding of the cost to society of this lost potential.

What is happening with our challenged youth? They feel they are not being heard and accepted. They are voting with their feet by not completing their education. We have been attempting to fit them into a small box of possibilities while they want to expand into the vastness of their potentiality. Instead of hearing the dreams and desires of these challenged yet talented kids, we have been telling them what they are to become. Many youth leave high school and college not knowing what they want. They may be discouraged from pursuing their dreams by those who have no dreams. They do not get engaged. They do not understand how the work they are doing in school applies to their lives.

In order to capture the passion of others, we must build emotional bonds. Brain research shows that all our decisions are made by routing sensory signals through the emotional part of the brain. If there is a compelling event, the brain can literally be hijacked by this most ancient part of our brain before the thinking brain has a chance to engage.

Almost 2/3 of our values and beliefs are formed before the age of five. Our emotional impressions and memories are based on emotions from our past. They create feelings and feelings create our thoughts. Research has shown that we are over 80% unconscious everyday. In most cases we do not realize that we are making decisions based on beliefs from the past that may or may not apply to the current situation. The way we think causes our behavior. Our behavior causes responses or reactions from others that either build up or tear down relationships. We then build successful or unsuccessful outcomes. The resulting cycle is the way we think becomes our habits of thought and these habits of thought become our attitudes.

Attitudes are a key component of emotional intelligence and play a major role in success. We can learn to be mindful and responsible for what we are thinking while making a choice for success thoughts. When we have negative thoughts that move us away from our goals, we can recognize them and choose differently. Developing a successful attitude becomes the preferred choice when we determine that we are responsible for choosing positive thoughts that move us closer to our goals.

Another key component of emotional intelligence is building relationships through compassion. We are not islands and we cannot reach our goals alone. For those children who are not taught how to build relationships, they may be ostracized from groups. Many are not taught to be compassionate and do not understand and value each other's differences. Children are taught to be competitive and may undermine each other as a matter of habit. All of this carries over into our adult life unless we learn how to overcome our relationship obstacles. However, when we are taught how to build relationships, we learn to recognize the value of each person. Even relationship-challenged youth can learn to engage with others to assist them to achieve their goals. It is a win - win for everyone involved.

A third key component is to build hope in us and in others by establishing goals. We want and need to have a vision and a purpose in our life. We want to understand what is important to us in the social, mental, physical, ethical, family and career areas of our life. These are the things that get us out of bed in the morning and that give us passion. These things will clarify for us what our values are. We can then establish what is important. By setting goals and moving toward them, we find hope. When we are hopeful, we find our joy. We can then play a part in helping others to be hopeful and to achieve their aspirations.

These concepts help to build strong leaders. There is a great need to educate our students about what it takes to make good life decisions. This can only be carried out by educators and parents who understand it themselves. So I repeat the question ... can we really expect our children to be good leaders if our educators and parents are not? When we do not understand the underlying basis for deciding what is a good choice and what is a bad choice, we have no method in place to help ourselves and others to recognize what is moving ourselves and others closer to the kind of life we want and what is moving us further away from it.

The Education and Economic Development Act is a South Carolina law that has a great deal of insight. It requires, in addition to several other significant provisions that character education be taught. When we build our educators into emotionally intelligent leaders with an emphasis on attitude, interpersonal skills and goal achievement, they will engage with students in their dreams and educate them in leadership skills. Then, we will truly have a totally engaged student population who are mindful of their attitudes, compassionate for others and have hope for their future.

## Chapter 21: Manage anger through empathy

Empathy is the ability to identify oneself emotionally in others, it is the key to being able to carry forward an important relationship and to live peacefully together. Some are born with a natural ability in this sense, while others have difficulty in relating to people. You can increase your sense of empathy in various ways if you realize you are not able to put yourself in another person's shoes. This chapter will talk about the meaning of empathy and will provide suggestions to become more empathetic.

Get in touch with your emotions. To be able to share an emotion with someone else you must first learn how to feel it. Is your heart lit? Do you notice that you are happy, sad, angry or scared? Express your feelings? You have to let them flow inside you and allow them to be part of your life, rather than repress them.

It is normal to try to remove negative thoughts. Nobody likes to sit down and think of sad events, it is much more fun to get distracted with the TV or go to the bar. The problem is that suppressing an emotion creates a sort of disconnection, a lack of familiarity with sensation. How can you think of being able to feel the sadness of others, if you are not able to express yours?

Reserve some time each day to allow emotions to emerge. Instead of trying to block negative feelings, learn more. Feel fear and anger, and deal with your emotions in a healthy way: cry, write your thoughts on a diary or talk to a friend.

Learn to listen. Listen carefully to what the other tells you, and notice his tone of voice. Observe it well and try to catch all the clues that can make you understand how it is. Note if your lip trembles and your eyes are shiny. It may also be less visible, maybe it looks down or looks absent. Put your questions aside and try to assimilate that person's story.

Avoid judging while listening. You may feel the need to criticize the choices made by that person, do not do it. If you notice distracting yourself, try to get back into listening mode.

Pretend to be the other person. Have you ever read an action story so exciting that you forget who you are? For a few minutes you can become the protagonist, can you imagine exactly what it means to see your father for the first time in ten years, or lose the love for the fault of another. When you listen to a person, if you try to understand her deeply, at a certain point you start to feel what she feels. You get an idea of what it means to wear your shoes.

Do not be afraid of feeling uncomfortable. Empathy can be painful! Absorbing another's pain hurts, and it takes a good effort to be able to bind on such a profound level. This is probably the level for which empathy is in decline: it is much easier to maintain a light conversation, to remain self-sufficient and safe. If you want to be more empathetic you can not escape people's emotions, which can have a strong impact on you. You might feel different at some point, but it's only because you deeply understood that person and laid the foundation for a solid relationship.

Feel compassion. Ask questions that show your interest. Use the body language to communicate a connection: look him in the eye, lean towards him, do not shake. Annuisci, shake your head and smile at the most appropriate moments. The other will stop sharing his emotions with you if you seem distracted, look away or show somehow that you are not interested.

Another way is to share yourself. Show the other that he is as vulnerable as he is, there will be a relationship of trust and a mutual connection between you. Lower the guard and participate in the conversation.

Use your empathy to help others. Being empathetic towards someone is an instructive experience, letting what you learn influence your actions in the future. The next time you see a guy haunted by a bully, maybe you will help him, because at that moment you will know how well he feels. It could change the way you behave when you know a new person, or your beliefs about certain social and political issues. Let empathy influence your way of life.

Always try to learn something new. Empathy arises from the desire to know people and their experiences. Try to find out everything you can about the lives of others. Set yourself the goal of getting to know the people around you as much as possible every day. Here are some tips to stimulate your curiosity:

Travel more. When you arrive at a place you've never visited, try to spend time with the locals to learn about their lifestyle.

Talk to strangers. If you're at the bus stop with someone, start a conversation instead of sticking your nose in a book.

Try empathy for people you do not like. If you notice any shortcomings in your empathic abilities, try to change towards or at least try to intimately understand the people and groups you do not like. Ask yourself why you feel revulsion for someone. Try to put yourself in his shoes instead of avoiding or insulting him. Find out what you can learn by experiencing empathy for unpleasant people.

## Conclusion

Having a significantly higher IQ is good for logical reasoning and other problem-solving skills, but without emotional intelligence to back that up, it often amounts to little or nothing. Recent research has shown that people with average IQs would often perform better and are more likely to be successful than individuals with high IQs. Daniel Goleman in his 1995 book, Emotional Intelligence, explains that the intelligence quotient only accounts for 20% of productivity, especially for those in leadership positions. Deductive and logical reasoning have their places in academic success and other accomplishments, but it takes a lot more to guarantee success in any area of life.

You would think that people with significant IQs, such as scientists, would be able to detach themselves from emotional bias, but this is not often the case. Unlike

IQ, which can be predetermined by genetics and other factors, EQ requires intention and repetition before it can be mastered. Even then, you have to keep checking to make sure your psychology is in perfect health.

It is my sincere hope that the information in this book has been of help in enlightening you about the necessity and benefits of emotional intelligence. Start working on the improvement of your EQ today, not only for your own happiness, but for the happiness of those in your life.

CPSIA information can be obtained
at www.ICGtesting.com
Printed in the USA
BVHW041046090720
583344BV00010B/809

9 781989 965290